MADE IN INVERNESS

A baby boomer's upbringing in the Highland Capital

Charles Bannerman

PUBLISHED BY

RBURKITT PUBLICATIONS

rburkitt4@gmail.com

Copyright Charles Bannerman October 2021

ISBN 978-1-7398078-0-1

Acknowledgements

My first thanks must go to the "Inverness Then And Now" and "Inverness, The City And Surrounding Highland Area" Facebook pages, because the love of all things Inverness that they radiate was my initial inspiration. And, as I pondered over whether or not to publish it, the enthusiasm and encouragement of their members made up my mind

For production, I went straight back to For The Right Reasons which had handled my other two most recent books. Unfortunately the charity was on the point of closing, but Richard Burkitt and Stewart Forbes have carried on in their own right as publishers and printers. Thank you both for getting this book on to the shelves.

My gratitude also goes to Jenny Bannerman, Stephen Mackay and Peter Marwick for setting up a mail order system which already promises to extend half way round the world.

As I write, sales outlets are still being finalised, but I was determined that this should sell somewhere on "home ground" in Dalneigh. And what better than just 100 yards from where I was brought up? I was absolutely delighted when Brian Duncan of the Dalneigh Stores in St Margarets Road (first known in the 60s as "Jocky Lawson's") so readily agreed to stock it. Others will emerge after this page is written

I must also acknowledge the many people who showed such moral support when they found out what I was doing, and one final and fundamental thank you must be to the people of Inverness who make the place what it is.

Contents:

PREFACE

Inspiration for this book came from discovering the passion for old Inverness, which shines through in various Facebook sites such as Inverness, Then And Now, and Inverness, The City and Surrounding Highland Area. They all admirably celebrate our heritage Apart from nourishing this interest, I also aim to provide a record of Inverness life during that third quarter of the 20th century.

This is Inverness according to just one person, but for Dalneigh you could read Old Hilton, the Merkinch, Raigmore and others. And, with a few modifications, for Inverness Royal Academy you could read Inverness High School or Millburn. Doing so immediately multiplies identification with the text. For instance, Pagliari's little ice cream van went all over the town and not only Academy pupils bought 3d single fags from Frankie Jew. This is not a Dalneigh book – it's an Inverness book with Dalneigh just a significant vehicle.

This is a snapshot of town life in a very different age, without more recent luxuries and sophistications, and without many of old Inverness's landmarks. But this is also Inverness to a generation who still, for instance, talk about the Caley, Station and Cumming's Hotels and about Kingsmills and Telford Street Parks.

One reaction which I fully expect is "You never mentioned X". There are two possible reasons for that – either that I didn't know about it because it wasn't among my personal experiences, or it was among the many things I had to leave out for lack of space. I have frequently opted for quantity over depth so I can pull as many memory strings as possible, but even then there's a limit.

I also expect to be told that I have made mistakes. When you mainly rely on your own memory going back several decades, the odd error will be inevitable. In the fortunate event of a second edition, I will attempt any corrections.

This is my seventh book about Inverness, and its predecessors are all devoted to local institutions. Four of these were the Up Stephen's Brae series about life at Inverness Royal Academy at Midmills. The others are Against All Odds, the official history of the merger creating Inverness Caledonian Thistle FC, and Maroon and Gold, the official history of Inverness Harriers. I hope that the nature of this volume makes it appeal to an even wider readership.

Finally, half a century has now elapsed since Pounds, Shillings and Pence gave way to decimal currency, so I probably need to give a short guide to the old money and Imperial units. There were 12 pennies in a shilling (also called a bob) and 20 shillings in a pound (or a quid). One decimal penny was therefore 2.4 old ones, making five to the shilling. In my earliest days, farthings (quarter of a penny) had just disappeared but there were still half pennies, threepenny bits, sixpences (tanners), two bob bits (sometimes called florins), half crowns (2s 6d or 12.5 decimal pennies) and ten bob notes.

Elsewhere, a foot is 12 inches, there are three of them in a yard and 1760 yards in a mile (1.609 km). A pound is 16 ounces, a stone 14 pounds, a hundred weight is eight stone and a ton (1.035 tonnes) consists of 20 hundredweights. Arithmetic is so much simpler these days!

Charles Bannerman, Inverness. Oct 2021.

THE AUTHOR

Charles Bannerman was born in the maternity wing of Inverness's old Raigmore Hospital and, apart from his two earliest years spent in Wick, and term time at University, has lived his entire life in the city.

He was educated at Dalneigh Primary School and Inverness Royal Academy before taking First Class Honours and the Crum Brown Medal for Chemistry at Edinburgh University in 1975. After a year of teacher training at Aberdeen College of Education he taught Maths at Millburn Secondary for a single session before transferring to the Chemistry Department at Inverness Royal Academy where he remained until his retiral in 2013.

Rather than seek promotion in teaching, he pursued a dual career in the classroom and in sports journalism. However, he did become a Senior Teacher in charge of the school's public relations in 1995. His journalistic career began as athletics correspondent with the Inverness Courier and also included, for 10 years, writing the Sportsview column in the Highland News.

However, most of his journalistic output has been in broadcasting and since 1984 he has serviced BBC local radio output for the Highlands and Islands with sports reports. When Scottish League football came to Inverness in 1994, he began almost 20 years of live match day reporting, initially for radio and latterly for television. He has also spent 10 years as BBC Scotland's match day shinty reporter. He has twice won the "Sportswriter of the Year" accolade at the Highland Media Awards and has also been Shinty Reporter of the Year.

His career as an author began in 1995 when he published "Up Stephen's Brae", the first of four volumes about life at Inverness Royal Academy. This was followed two years later by "Against All Odds", the official account of the football merger which created Inverness Caledonian Thistle. In 2014 he produced "Maroon and Gold", the official history of Inverness Harriers.

He has two children – Jenny who is one of his several international athletes and Martin who is Audit Director with a local firm of Chartered Accountants.

Running is one of his main leisure activities and he still manages to get out around four or five times a week.

CHAPTER 1 – FIRST STEPS IN INVERNESS.

Although born and almost entirely brought up in the place, my Inverness credentials are not quite perfect since three of my four grandparents originate from further north. However, it was on the banks of the River Ness that I was most certainly forged into the person I eventually became. Whilst warmly acknowledging with some pride the Caithness part of my heritage, I therefore regard myself fundamentally as an Invernessian.

My father, George Bannerman, was like myself, born in the Highland Capital - in 1920 on Shore Street where the family lived at number 7 then 35. My paternal grandmother, Catherine Fraser, was Inverness through and through but my grandfather, also George, was a railwayman from Wick.

In 1932 the Highland Railway moved my grandfather back to Wick and he spent the next 30 years mainly on that long and tortuous far north line, often battering snow drifts out of the way. Drivers' duties ranged from delivering the aristocracy to their estates to leaving pints of milk at every tiny station that trains still stopped at. If the rail trip to Wick and Thurso is a lengthy one today, it was far worse then.

My dad became Dux of the Bell's School in Farraline Park in 1932 and won a bursary for Inverness Royal Academy, which he was unable to take up. The family move led to the rest of his upbringing in Wick and a short spell working as a reporter with the John O'Groat Journal before an early military call-up in 1939 due to his membership of the Territorial Army.

On my mother's side my grandfather, who died

in 1946 so I never knew him, was an engineer from Wick while my granny's family were ropemakers from Canisbay on the far north coast. There are quite long generations on that side of the family and they were both born in 1879. She lived with us until she died in 1965 so I am fortunate enough to have been told first hand stories of what it was like to grow up in rural Caithness in the 1880s.

My parents met at Wick High School and married in 1942. Days later my dad, after training and service in the UK, sailed off with the rest of the re-formed 51st Highland Division to participate in the remaining three years of Adolf Hitler's downfall. This started at the Battle of El Alamein, leading to the eviction of Erwin Rommel from North Africa, and continued through Sicily, France, Belgium, Holland and Germany, ending up in Cuxhaven.

After he was demobbed in 1946, my dad passed Civil Service exams and became a Tax Officer in the Inland Revenue in Wick. An only child, I was born in July 1953, but my mother was taken to Raigmore Hospital in Inverness for the birth, thus securing that part of my Invernessian heritage.

Early in 1954, the house the family owned in Wick's Kinnaird Street was scheduled for demolition as part of a redevelopment so we moved to Leith Walk and a Swedish house not dissimilar to the one we acquired in Dalneigh four years later. My father's promotion to Tax Officer Higher Grade in 1955 led to a move to Inverness soon after, so my earliest memories of Wick are pretty few and far between.

I just remember the Leith Walk house and one or two neighbours, as well as the dog which tried to steal my biscuit and nipped my finger in the process. This trauma gave me a lifelong apprehension about dogs, so it must have been before this incident that my mother emerged from a shop to find me still in my push chair but holding on like grim death to the tail of some hapless canine. In the 1950s, it was nothing unusual to leave children briefly unattended outside shops.

I also retain a vague image of standing on the kitchen table, watching a rescue helicopter landing in the North School playground as part of Operation Snowdrop during the extremely hard winter of 1955. This was the only way of supporting remote settlements inundated by heavy snow where the people conveyed their needs by tracing a letter in the snow using ashes from the fire - F for food, D for doctor and so on.

After several weeks' delay, the family moved south and, for the few days it took to complete the flitting, I was sent to stay with my aunt and uncle in one of the former Admiralty Cottages in Invergordon. These were the dying days of Invergordon as a naval base and I just remember large grey ships in the Cromarty Firth, although trips to the Admiralty Playing Fields to watch my uncle playing cricket continued when we later came to visit.

My parents travelled to Inverness by train while the flitting went by road and my aunt took me to a level crossing in Invergordon to wave to them onwards through the soot and steam.

Our first house in Inverness was Catriona Villa at 93, Kenneth Street, a rented upper floor apartment on the corner of Ross Avenue, not far from the horse trough which still sat at the end of Wells Street. I seem to have lived fairly dangerously there since I contracted whooping cough and got an electric shock from a plug with the fairly primitive safety features of the time.

On a very hot day in the summer of 1956, I also managed to sit down in the middle of newly tarred Ross Avenue and the pitch black, semi-molten hydrocarbon stuck remorselessly to my legs and clothes. The trousers were binned and my mother eventually got the tar off my legs with liberal applications of butter. It would be another decade and a half before I would realise that the key to this folk remedy was the non-polar nature of both materials, making the tar soluble enough in the butter for it to ease away from the skin.

As most young children do, I had a special cuddly toy - a rabbit which went everywhere with me. I was already developing an unfortunate lifelong penchant for complicated words and my mother had been telling me about how they were using disease to control the rabbit population in places like Australia. I probably didn't fully understand that, but I do seem to have picked up enough to go into a nearby butcher's shop with my rabbit and announce, with my still marked lisp, that it had "myxthomatothith".

Our stay at number 93 was brief and my parents' ultimate aim was to acquire a council house. However, these were still in short supply and subject to a waiting list, despite massive post-war building programmes - in Inverness at Hilton and Dalneigh in particular. We therefore moved a few yards down Kenneth Street to number 70 - Carron Cottage, which was owned by Mary Jane Campbell, retired infant mistress at Merkinch School. Mary Jane herself was by now in Rossal, then an Old Folks' Home (a title long since superseded by the more euphemistic "Care Home") and was renting out her house.

It was quite a large ground floor property with a big garden and a disused wash house, in both of which I spent a lot of time playing. There were three bedrooms, a living room off the small kitchen and also "the front room" - a sanctum sanctorum which, in accordance with normal practice, was never used for family purposes but instantly swung into action if there were visitors, or especially if the Minister arrived. The Best China was also kept in there.

I was now old enough to remember more of what transpired, such as sitting out on the kerb with my feet dangling into the Kenneth Street gutter. This was still the main A9 from Inverness to Dingwall and the far north, but traffic was pretty light and a three or four year old sitting out there wasn't regarded as risky.

It seems that sitting out on the pavement also helped me develop my vocabulary from what I heard from passers by. For on one occasion my mother was just coming down the path to take me back inside when, to her horror, she heard me advise one pedestrian that "it's a b****r of a day today"! It probably wasn't, because I was just repeating by rote what I had heard on the street.

One crystal clear recollection of an unusual visit to the front room is of a winter afternoon with leaden clouds enveloping the town. Making its silent way through ever deepening snow on Kenneth Street was an orange horse drawn Stratton milk float whose driver at that time of day must have been collecting his money. Another memory of that room I cannot explain because it involves my first Airfix model, a Heinkel III, and it is inconceivable that I would have been allowed polystyrene cement at all, never mind anywhere near my mother's "good suite".

The former Burgh Police Station, Castle Wynd.

The ambience of 70, Kenneth Street - its furniture, decor, kitchen equipment and so on - significantly pre-dated the 1950s. Mary Jane Campbell must have kept a fairly anachronistic home. The kitchen in particular was like something out of Downton Abbey with virtually no mod cons and the classic double sink. It was the standard one deep, one shallow arrangement for washing clothes when washing machines were still very uncommon.

The glass surfaced washing board was placed in a central position and I can still hear the unique, rhythmic rasping sound as my mother used sheer friction to force the dirt out of our clothes.

My granny, now almost 80, liked to make herself feel useful and insisted on doing much of the cooking. Sometimes this could be hit or miss, but her soups - lentil, tattie, broth - were a delight and improved as they matured from first to second to third day of consumption. With a refrigerator still many years distant, the mind boggles at some of the biochemistry which could have been in operation by that third day in particular! She also did a superb line in slightly burnt mince and tatties which I always mixed with my fork into a paste – and still do.

Supplementing that staple 1950s diet were some legacies of a wartime Welfare Food scheme which had been continued into the next decade. National Dried Milk came as powder in large white tins with distinctive blue labelling and was quite palatable. Less so was the cod liver oil for which you had to brace yourself as your mother approached your mouth with the spoon. As a source of Vitamin C she also bought Haliborange tablets from the chemist.

It was in this house, at Christmas 1957, that I experienced the joy of my first tricycle - universally known as a trike. Smuggled into the house under my very nose and without me ever questioning how Santa got such a bulky object down the chimney, this was a blue and white Vindec model. It became my pride and joy at a time when kids' toys were generally pretty primitive and seldom much more elaborate than tin soldiers or Dinky cars.

For the next part of this story we must move on several months, because I am told that it was mid-

MacKintosh's lemonade bottles

summer when no one was remotely thinking of Christmas. I was sitting at the dining table in that back living room and suddenly announced "Mum.... there isn't really a Santa - is there?" I was just turning five... and the myth had been blown!

On the subject of chimneys, coal fires were still commonplace, so these needed swept. Jack Fraser, with his bubbling personality and iconic dirty face, lived on Argyle Street and plied his trade right across the town from a van. I was absolutely intrigued when I was taken outside to see his brush pop out of the chimney pot. That might be more problematic if you had a cowl – a curved metal structure on top of the chimney, designed to rotate away from the wind to stop smoke blowing back down into the room, which made it smell for quite some time.

The other occupation which went with a black face was the coalman. With their backs protected by thick leather waistcoats, these hardy souls used brute strength to transfer hundredweight sacks from lorry to coal bunker where they would empty them with a resounding crunch. A whole day of that must have been hard work indeed. There were several coal merchants in Inverness, including Fraser's not far along the road but my mother used McGruther and Marshall. Every month we would go into their Dickensian office in station square to "pay the account" as detailed on the small handwritten paper bill which arrived by post.

Two sets of neighbours played an especially prominent part in my early social life. Straight across the road there was the Johnston family and I played a lot with their kids Ian and Margaret, with whom I also went to Sunday School. And then, two doors down from us at number 66, there were the elderly sisters, Miss Paterson and the widowed Mrs MacKintosh. My mother was very friendly with them both and they got on very well with me so we used to spend a fair time in their house and garden.

Mrs MacKintosh had married into the local lemonade dynasty of that name whose factory was on Abban Street. MacKintosh's lemonade was a local institution and probably outsold Hays, Sangs, Cruickshanks and Bob Accord. They did a number of different flavours ranging from the orthodox such as cola, plain and orange through to a delicious creation of their own known as Queen's Cup, complete with an image of Windsor Castle on the label.

In the 1950s lemonade bottles, on which you paid a 3d deposit, were still at a fairly early stage of evolution. MacKintosh's ones were of a stout glass variety with the company name embossed on them and the stoppers were made of a kind of black stone material which screwed into the neck, with a rubber washer ensuring gas tightness. I used to have the masochistic habit of rubbing the stone stopper against my teeth which truly set them on edge.

There was no question of my mother going out to work, even though my granny could have provided adequate child care. Relatively few wives worked and for some families - including my own - it was regarded as something of a status symbol if the wife stayed at home. They did have the option of sending me to a kindergarten but my mother was also a firm believer that, until school age, my daytime upbringing and education were her responsibility.

There was therefore no shortage of interpersonal contact and we went a lot of places together, notably "over the town", which was an Invernessism that she never quite came to terms with. We would not, of course, go on a Wednesday afternoon since that was early closing day, and there was virtually no Sunday trade at all. It was outside Wm. Low's in High Street that I suffered the traumatic ignominy of being violently sick all over the pavement, an experience so unpleasant that for years I was put off eating pineapple, overconsumption of which was blamed for the incident.

Lows was just one of several shops with old fashioned awnings to protect them from sunlight. In this pre-supermarket age, the town centre was full of shops, including two Camerons, both outfitters. This sometimes caused confusion since Alex Cameron was on the corner of High Street and Castle Street while F.A. Cameron was just 100 yards away in Church Street.

A visit to F.A. Cameron's was always a fascination since they had pneumatic tubes through which money and change whizzed to and fro between counter and cash office. The highlight of the process came right at the end when the container with the change arrived back with a sudden terminal "pop". Then in other shops, like Coopers with its unique old fashioned grocer's aroma, cash and change swung to and fro in containers suspended on wires. Contactless payment long before its time?

More fascinating still was "Hughie Pram's" in the Queensgate Market Arcade. Run by brothers Hugh and Duncan MacKenzie, this shop's most conspicuous outward feature was the prams and push chairs in which it did a roaring trade. But for a young child, Hughie Pram's was also a wonderland of toys, and a visit was always to be cherished. The brothers had a wonderful way with children who were not uncommonly very reluctant to leave the premises. One of many coffee shops, mainly under Italian ownership, was the Queensgate Cafe, but that's not what I used to call it. I had become interested in different makes of cars and outside these premises I spotted a Sunbeam Talbot, a marque which had quite recently gone out of production. From then on I would only call the place "The Queensgate Talbot" and still think of it as such.

One of my mother's favourite places for a cup of tea was The Carlton in Inglis Street.

Inverness Town House. The fleche on top is long gone

It was also a pub but during the day, middle class ladies who still perhaps felt a little uncomfortable in the stuffier precincts of the Caledonian Hotel, would gather there. As much of the hospitality industry modernised, this old world establishment was possibly one of the last in Inverness to continue with waitresses wearing black dresses, white aprons and white lace headgear.

If we felt like a longer trip in the summer, the delightful and greatly missed cafe in the Ness Islands was a further pleasant stop over. Also greatly missed in these Islands is the amphitheatre which used to host everything from roller skating to dancing. Another fairly upmarket eatery was Burnetts restaurant on the upper floor of the old Royal Academy building in Academy Street where ladies who predominantly didn't work could also relax after, for instance, a perm in Fornari the hairdressers across the road.

Burnetts was just one of a small army of local bakers in Inverness which have disappeared as alarmingly as the town's Italian cafes. Munro's, King's and Bowman's are all long gone, as is Anderson's ("Been Doing Our Best for You Since 1892" as it said on their vans) at the bottom of Academy Street. Then there was The Balmoral, and a great favourite was Skinner's, one of whose two shops was very popular with Royal Academy pupils passing it on their way up Stephen's Brae. Each had their own specialities – Cream Cookies, Fruit Slices, Apple Tarts and even the humble Morning Roll.

Although I had committed the sacrilege of Santa Denial, this didn't prevent my mother from taking me to see the man himself when he set up house in the winter wonderland they created in Benzie and Miller in Union Street. For half a crown you would get to sit on Santa's knee and tell him what you wanted for Christmas (which I must have done without a whiff of conscience about knowing he was a fake) and you also got quite a substantial wrapped present.

Benzie and Miller quickly became an Inverness institution after opening there in the early 1950s. The site was previously occupied by the outfitters Young and Chapman, which had an enviable local pedigree, but they sold out to Aberdeen based Benzie and Miller in 1952, causing a major rift in the Young family.

However the feature of an Inverness Christmas that most people of this era best remember was the delightful Disney artwork in the Playhouse cinema cafe. This wonderland of Snow Whites and Bambis and Donald Ducks was the brainchild of the cinema's manager Jimmy Nairn who was also a renowned producer of home movies, many of which provide an excellent historical record of Inverness. Disneyland brought kids and parents into the cafe in their hundreds and when the building burned down in 1972 there was more than the loss of a cinema.

Dominating the opposite end of Academy Street was the imposing grey bulk of the gasometer with its slatted wooden outer shell. Before North Sea Gas, every town had its own gas works where coal was roasted to drive off a gaseous mixture with a large component of carbon monoxide, leaving behind coke. It was this carbon monoxide that made coal gas extremely poisonous and hence also a not infrequent means of suicide. Sometimes you could just catch a whiff of that mysterious odour of coal distillation if you walked close by. The gasometer held the town's supply of gas which was then pumped into mains.

Two other features of that end of the town were auditory. The Rose Street Foundry was a well established workplace in Inverness and in 1944 was famously involved in the PLUTO project – a welded Pipe Line Under The Ocean to carry fuel from the UK to the Normandy invasion beaches. It then changed its name to Resistance Welders and again to AI Welders. Known widely in Inverness simply as The Welders, the works had a loud siren to mark the end of shifts which could be heard all over town. And then there was the 8 o'clock bell – a relic of the days of curfew which sounded every evening from the Old High Church. I did not, however, hear that for some time since I was invariably sound asleep by 8pm.

Bellfield Park was another place of wonderment. In 1956, a new paddling pool was opened in one corner and proved a huge hit with kids, both locals and a still limited number of visitors. On a summer afternoon this was a real treat, and so was an ice cream from the pavilion where you could buy tickets and hire equipment for the tennis courts, table tennis and two putting greens. Apart from an upgrade of the swings and other attractions and the addition of a bandstand, this iconic Inverness attraction has only seen limited change in over 50 years.

Quite often we would go for walks to more local shops or round nearby streets. Late on a winter afternoon, the gas lights which still illuminated a number of streets would come on. By then this was without the assistance of the town's squad of "leeries" whose job it had been to light them manually in earlier years.

I was quite bemused at the number of houses which had low front walls, with strange metallic stumps sticking out of them. My mother tried to explain that the stumps were where iron railings had been cut away to provide metal for making ships and tanks during the war but, although little over a decade in the past, the concept of that conflict was still beyond me. These metal stumps were a very common feature of the post-war years, especially in more affluent areas where more houses had had railings, and some can still be seen.

One of the less affluent parts was Duff Street where many of the houses were in a dreadful state of repair and a lot of people still lived in what, even to this young child, was an obvious state of squalor. My mum couldn't help but notice me recoiling at some of the sights, and indeed the next time I misbehaved she threatened me with going to live in Duff Street!

Of particular fascination was Grieg Street which links Kenneth Street with the Greig Street Bridge, a crossing built in the 1880s to allow the growing population of the area, known as the Big Green, easier access to the town centre and vice versa. Greig Street was a place of wonder with all manner of shops and businesses, most notably, at my age, Salvadori's cafe which was certainly one of many candidates for the source of Inverness's best ice cream.

This was one of several Italian cafes in Inverness, such as the Locarno, the Ness Cafe and Dorando's, and it was run by old Mr Salvadori with some help from his son Vaaro - and also from his daughters who were a considerable magnet for the local young men. Helping them was a great character called Mrs Mitchell who worked behind the counter. You had the option of raspberry cordial on your ice cream and also of taking it away or eating it in one of the shop's booths. Frequently we would opt for the latter and my mother would have a coffee.

Salvadori's was just a sample of what the Greig Street shopping precinct had to offer. Jimmy Munro, who sang in our church choir, had a grocer's and there was Mr Cushnie's post office, a pharmacy and a Coop. Frank Hill ran the newsagent where my dad got his papers and, more importantly for me, my weekly Harold Hare comic.

Across the road was Mr Baddon's bike shop where my dad bought a smart green model and fitted a leather seat on the bar for me. One day when we were turning from Huntly Street on to the suspension bridge, he lost his balance and we both fell off. My dad cut his head and I was predictably crying but was soothed with a sweetie from a passerby. Strangely enough, three decades later this was a bedtime story I used to tell my son Martin and used to receive frequent requests for repeats. I have also told it to my grandchildren.

Be a cut above the rest!

Come to

DIGGER'S

for personal and efficient service

DIGGER'S

GREIG STREET, INVERNESS

————★————

ALL THE BEST FROM "DIGGER"

There were other shops on Greig Street, but none as memorable as Diggar the Barber's. Gilbert "Diggar" MacGillivray was a 14th Army Burma Star artillery veteran who had set up as an army barber at Fort George after the war, before opening his own shop in Greig Street. Far larger than life, Diggar was a one man institution and had the capacity to talk incessantly, a talent he frequently used to the full.

Everyone who came into that shop received the Gospel according to Diggar, as did many who did not since he was quite capable of abandoning his customer in mid cut to dash to his front door and hurl good natured abuse at this passer by or that. One frequent recipient was John Brooman, a leading light in Caledonian FC of which Diggar was a passionate supporter. Diggar also completed the Bluenose double through an equally fervent dedication to Rangers.

Indeed, when Caley merged with Thistle in 1993, Diggar had quite recently died. One of the leading "rebels" opposing the move was John Brooman's grandson who solemnly declared in a radio interview: "Diggar McGillivray is barely cold in his grave, and look what they're doing to the club!"

Diggar's parallel line of business was as a football pools agent and another frequent source of interruption to your haircut was the arrival of a series of punters who needed supplied with their Littlewoods, Vernons or Zetters coupons.

The time interval between entering and leaving Diggar's shop could be considerable. The experience (and that it was) began with a seat on a bench running the length of the back wall and reading a generous supply of The Beano, The Dandy and Commando comics whilst waiting to be attended to. During the wait, you could get up to date with a lot of Desperate Dan, Lord Snooty and The Bash Street Kids. Eventually, with your visit frequently punctuated by coupon purchasers and pauses for Diggar to speak to (or indeed at) people, you would leave with your short back and sides, administered with his smaller customers seated on a board across the chair arms. For years, certainly until I left for university, I would let no one else cut my hair - except for Diggar's son Dennis who also became involved in the business.

The famously verbose Diggar, who lived on Ballifeary Road, once attended a local residents' meeting to discuss energy supply. The previously staid proceedings allegedly dissolved into spontaneous hilarity when Diggar advised the gathering: "But of course, I'm all gas!"

One feature of Inverness which my mother never came to terms with was how frequently the streets are dug up, something which was much less common in Wick. Some things never change, and frequently abandoned road works remain prominent in the city.

The disastrous Suez Crisis of 1956, horribly mismanaged by Anthony Eden who conspired with Israel and France to invade the Canal Zone and was then told to get out by US President Eisenhower, had its implications on the home front. It led to fuel rationing which Ministry of Transport driving examiners were redeployed to oversee, so tests were suspended. Learner drivers were therefore temporarily allowed on the road unaccompanied and one of the beneficiaries was my namesake, my Uncle Charlie in Invergordon. He had just bought his first car, a dark green A30, and was allowed to take it straight out on his own, at which point there began a series of visits between our families, ultimately in both directions, which lasted for over 50 years.

The number of Invernessians who can remember the town's third cinema, the Palace, is by now dwindling because it became a bingo hall early in 1963. Since it was quite close to home, my mother would sometimes take me there of an afternoon and it was here that I first met Jimmy Edwards as "Whacko!". This was a series about a larger than life school teacher where hostility to and the caning of pupils was actually the central theme and the main comic device of the plot. Another film I saw there, also in black and white, was Lorna Doone, but when John Ridd, played by Richard Greene, later of Robin Hood fame, started kissing the eponymous heroine, I

29

stood up in my seat and shouted something along the lines of "Stop that and get on with it!"

Sometimes on a Friday, when he finished at 4:30, we would go and meet my dad as he cycled home from work. The Inland Revenue office was in the large Government Building at the far end of Longman Road, and any time he took me in there was a great event, especially if I was allowed to use the official ink stamps and the paper punch. But on Fridays we would just walk as far as the humped railway bridge at Railway Terrace and wait for him there. This, however, was not the start of the weekend since a five and a half day week also saw the Civil Service work on Saturday mornings.

One less appealing activity with my mother was afternoon visits to one or other of her friends. It was extremely boring to a four year old to sit in someone's front room and listen to a couple of women chinwagging as they drank tea. One such destination was Mrs Reid's in Charles Street. This was the wife of one of my dad's old army mates who comprised much of my parents' circle of friends for many years. Every so often we would head down Kenneth Street, Tomnahurich Street and Young Street towards the suspension bridge. Bridge Street and the Raining Stairs then quickly got us to Charles Street and quite a boring afternoon.

However it was these visits to Mrs Reid that brought me my first experience of an institution which, above all others, has played a central role in my life. On one occasion I asked the ladies who were these big boys and girls walking up the street in blue jackets, some of them with yellow stuff round them - and the genie was out of the bottle. This was my first experience of Inverness Royal Academy.

Shortly after, in June 1958, we all went to the Academy playing field on Victoria Drive to watch Mrs Reid's son Alan in the school sports, and that was another seminal moment if there ever was one. Not only was this my first visit to a playing field which would within a decade become so important to me, it was also my first experience of competitive athletics.

When we moved into 70, Kenneth Street, it was on the understanding that this was an interim measure pending a council house in Dalneigh. However, Mary Jane Campbell had promised my parents that, during her lifetime at least, we would never be evicted until we had found somewhere. But Mary Jane was by now quite infirm and it was clear that her beneficiaries were less understanding and indeed on one occasion my mother was obliged to advise them of our rights in no uncertain terms.

All the same, the race was on to acquire that Dalneigh house and my dad was a frequent visitor to Mr Attwater of the Housing Department, based in the Parish Council Offices on Bank Street, where Johnny Foxes now is. He would often take me with him, although for some months to no avail.

Since we knew we would be moving sooner or later, I was enrolled in Dalneigh Primary School in the spring of 1958 with a view to starting Primary 1 that August. The alternative would have been Central School and then to move after a very short time. I have the clearest recollection of that walk from Kenneth Street via Rowan Road to the school for enrolment. I then covered some of the road home with huge exaggerated steps since I was now a "big boy" and going to school.

The woman who enrolled me was Dalneigh's formidable Infant Mistress, Miss Kate MacLean -

white haired when she didn't have a purple rinse, and with a trademark perm. Kate had been appointed to a similar job at the Royal Academy primary department in 1946 but when that was phased out during the latter 50s, she became surplus to requirement along with other colleagues and was redeployed to the then new school at Dalneigh.

Kate was a unique mixture. She had a heart of gold and could be kindness personified, but at the same time could be roused to anger by miscreants and thought nothing of applying the belt to a five or six year old palm.

In the end we were not evicted but it was a close run thing. Mary Jane died very soon after we were eventually allocated a house in Dalneigh and we moved to 14, St Andrew Drive in October 1958.

My mother had to walk me to and from school for these first two months before we moved but in effect I had the simultaneous experiences of settling into a new school a new home and a new neighbourhood all at the same time.

These were changes which marked the beginning of a completely new and extremely fruitful stage of life.

CHAPTER 2 – DALNEIGH DEBUT.

One Saturday afternoon in October 1958 I walked with my parents, who had just received the keys to our new house, from Kenneth Street to St Andrew Drive. We came in through St Ninian Drive and "the garages" just off it, because from there you could quickly access our back gate.

Well, the house didn't actually have a back gate. That was something that my dad had to make and erect for himself because there was just a stricken concrete pillar and an eight foot gap between the minister's hedge and the end of one of the garage blocks. And it was there, playing some game or another, that I encountered the first of very many friends and acquaintances I would have in Dalneigh over the next fourteen years.

14, St Andrew Drive in 2021. I lived longer in that house than in any other. The tree is a newcomer.

Philip and Willie Crook, then aged five and four, were the second and third of five brothers who lived across the road from us at number 15. Ralph, the oldest, who 20 years later went on to open a hairdresser's shop in Castle Street, would have been going on 10, Michael was barely a toddler and Chris the youngest, who also opened a hairdresser's, was born round about this time. By strange coincidence, more than 40 years later, Chris's son and my daughter became friends and school mates at the Royal Academy.

With the benefit of hindsight, the yawning gap and the crumbling post at the back gate were an omen. For when we then walked through the front door, my parents jaws just dropped at the abomination which awaited us within. The previous family, who had moved to Heatherley Crescent, had left behind an absolute pigsty.

Graffiti on the walls.... lipstick writing all over an abandoned mirror ... filthy surfaces throughout.... junk strewn throughout the place and an all-pervading ambience of squalor. I had no idea that people actually lived in conditions like this, and it was going to be a major undertaking for my parents to clean and tidy this cesspit before they could organise a flitting.

This was what was known as a "Swedish house". It was made of wood and there were 100 of them at this end of Dalneigh and over 60 on the far side of the school. Half of them were mirror images of the others; some four in a block and others, like ours, semi-detached. However most Dalneigh dwellings were of harled brick, ranging from semi-detached to long terraces.

Nowadays these Swedish houses are mainly dark

brown outside but initially they were for a while yellow, otherwise grey. This was why, at the height of Beatlemania in the mid-60s, some Dalneigh kids could be heard to sing "We all live in a yellow Swedish house".

On entering the front door of our right hand semi, you faced a stairs going straight up the end wall. Parallel with that was a short corridor leading to the downstairs bathroom with a square frosted window and there was a large cupboard under the stairs. The living room door was on the left and at the back of the house was a kitchen large enough for a dining table. As in Kenneth Street there were two sinks, shallow and deep, for washing clothes. To begin with, I was still small enough to fit into the large one to avoid running a full bath. Towards the back door there was another large cupboard with the hot water tank, and three smaller ones.

The long master bedroom was at the top of the stairs above the kitchen and the other two were at the front. One had a window which you could climb directly out of on to the roof of the porch and the other, directly above the living room, had a grate for a fire. Like the one in the living room immediately below it, this was tiled in the classic style of the era.

Coal fires were pretty well universal, and I was often roused in the morning by the sound of my mother downstairs scraping out the previous day's ashes and laying the new fire. A bed of newspapers and kindling sticks, about half an inch in cross section and six inches long, was laid first and the coal – quite a difficult fuel to set alight – was set on top. If there was any problem igniting the coal, and you didn't want to risk adding paraffin, you could place a sheet of newspaper on the top half of the opening so the incoming air would "draw" better through the bottom. Sometimes that would result in the panic of the paper going up in flames.

Beside every fire was a companion stand containing a poker, a brush and a small shovel. There were various kinds of coal – anthracite, Shilbottle, messy bituminous coal and so on – which all produced soot to a greater or lesser extent. This meant you needed to get your chimney swept periodically and if you waited too long there was the danger of your "lum going up". Chimney fires sometimes resolved themselves when the soot burned out but not infrequently the Fire Brigade had to be called. There was no difficulty locating the house since it would have a dense plume of black or grey smoke belching out of the "lum", which was very embarrassing for the householder.

Our garden was a bit bigger than many others. The back lawn was 10 yards long and before the wall of the garage block there was also a large bed of soil. Across the garden path was an equally extensive area where my dad grew potatoes, carrots, peas and a fair bit else. There was no shed but he built that as soon as he could after the priority of a gate (which is still there!). The shed was built out of the wood from boxes in which matches had been delivered to Brooman the wholesaler who was glad to get rid of the surplus containers.

At three corners of the lawn were poles from which was suspended a triangular arrangement of washing lines for drying clothes. The lines themselves were by now coated in white plastic and after my mother hung the wet clothes on them using wooden clothes pegs, she would raise the lines to the four winds by applying a "stretcher".

This was a long pole with a notch in the top to catch the line on before extending it upwards and was also often used by me as a weapon during re-enactments of Sir Lancelot. If it was too wet to put clothes out on the line, then the kitchen was equipped with a "pulley", a wooden frame on which the garments could be hung at waist level before being raised to the ceiling by a rope.

The Dalneigh council housing scheme, like its Hilton counterpart across the river, played a major part in Inverness's answer to the serious housing shortage which engulfed the country after the war. People were literally squatting in former army camps and living in caravans, while the more fortunate might have been lucky enough to acquire a "prefab".

These, as their nickname suggests, were prefabricated dwellings, very basic but adequate, which were delivered to sites in sections for quick assembly. They were erected in a few parts of Inverness such as near the Clach Park and one of my dad's former army comrades lived in one so I have memories of being inside what I initially called a "freefab".

By the mid-1950s Dalneigh, which extended west towards the Caledonian Canal from Dochfour Drive, had become a large and vibrant council housing scheme, straddling its own school and church which were the centre of the community. The school took its first pupils in 1954 but wasn't officially opened for another three years. The church dates from 1951 and its first minister, Rev Hamish MacIntyre, stayed for 20 years. He had been a founder member of the Iona Community just before the war and was extremely well liked in Dalneigh. The scheme was built on what had been Dalneigh

Farm whose name is of Gaelic origin and the farmhouse became the church manse.

The half dozen or so streets on the opposite side of the school from us were almost all named after trees - Lilac Grove, Maple Avenue, Rowan Road and so on. Meanwhile our part was well and truly canonised with the likes of St. Mungo Road, and St. Ninian, St. Andrew and St. Fergus Drives. Our street was frequently and wrongly apostrophised by the uninitiated, and we would often receive letters addressed to 14, St Andrew's Drive. Indeed one of its current official street signs still carries that very error, although someone has whitewashed out the "apostrophe-s".

The epicentre of that southern part of Dalneigh was the manse which had three different streets running round it and our garden was one of perhaps around 20 that backed on to its extensive policies.

These saintly thoroughfares were named after Biblical or Scottish religious figures, with one conspicuous exception which was also the longest street in that part of Dalneigh. Running parallel with the line of the canal was St Valery Avenue which has over 150 houses in it and a new street, St Valery Park, has since been built behind part of it.

Although also commemorating a "Saint", this street was poignantly named after St Valery en Caux in Northern France, where much of the 51st Highland Division had been captured by Rommel in June 1940. This was still very prominent in the Inverness psyche when these houses were erected and Inverness would also adopt a town twinning arrangement with St Valery.

There was perhaps a bit of socio-economic segregation in that Dalneigh scheme and some streets, including St Andrew Drive, had quite a large presence of middle class families. Rents in some streets were also said to be higher. However, the lack of shops near Dalneigh's extremities would not be addressed for some years.

Urban demography in the 1950s and 60s was quite different from what it is now because only a small number of families owned their own home. Areas like the Crown and around Fairfield Road abounded with large town houses, occupied by the better heeled, and mainly the product of the phenomenal building boom in Inverness during the last two decades of the 19th century. However Drakies, Lochardil, Scorguie and Holm Mains didn't exist at that time, far less Castle Heather or Culduthel Mains or Mile End.

This meant that many middle class families with a professional breadwinner were still housed in areas like Dalneigh and what is now called Old Hilton. As the 20th century progressed, so did the availability of mortgages and this created movement out of council schemes, led by these middle classes. This demography also had educational implications which we will look at in a later chapter.

So in its infancy Dalneigh had a genuinely mixed population, even though it appeared that the Council was operating a degree of internal segregation. During my time in St Andrew Drive, that 32 house street alone had three teachers, including a primary head teacher, the Burgh Architect, the Airport Manager and at least five middle management civil servants, including my father. But even by the time we moved out in 1972, the balance had already begun to change as families - predominantly middle class ones - moved to addresses like Drumossie

Avenue, Drumblair Crescent or Scorguie Road.

Dalneigh's great artery was Laurel Avenue, running from Caledonian Road right through to Bruce Gardens. Why Laurel Avenue is a dual carriageway, I have never been able to establish. I wondered if it had possibly been conceived as a link between the A82 at Glenurquhart Road and the A9 at Telford Street, but it's difficult to see how access and egress could have been achieved at its ends.

Until the early 60s, Laurel Avenue, which is a fair distance from several Dalneigh streets, also had the scheme's only shops, four in number including a Post Office and Alecky MacKenzie the grocer. This block, with houses on its upper floor, is also pretty well identical to a roughly contemporary facility in Hilton. To a lesser extent, the two schemes' primary schools also have structural similarities.

Laurel Avenue was a bit of a strange mix because at its far end, near the Bruce Gardens junction, there were a few families where certain members harboured what might be called aggressive tendencies. My main route home from secondary school or the town was up Dalneigh Road which crossed Laurel Avenue at the roundabout, just a few yards from the enclave in question. On approaching this junction, I would frequently pedal or walk just that bit faster, or even break into a trot. Indeed at least once I had to cycle for all I was worth in the interests of self preservation.

Inevitably these early years in Dalneigh were spent either under parental supervision or at school, which deserves a chapter of its own. Despite more liberal attitudes to allowing children out and about independently or with friends, this would have to wait for a year or two. My mother and I used to take the same kind of jaunts as from Kenneth Street, although longer because the town centre was now further away. But much of my activity was focused on our new house, which was very quickly transformed into a very habitable condition.

For someone with no formal training, my dad was pretty good at DIY, which for economic reasons was probably more of a way of life in the late 1950s. Apart from building the shed and the back gate he also decorated pretty well the entire house quite quickly. I very soon discovered the difference between the smells of oil paint, emulsion paint and wallpaper paste.

Come the spring of 1959, the garden was also transformed into flower beds at the front and vegetable patches at the back. Both areas had their neat lawns, kept in order by a mower which only had brute strength to move it and created a unique whirring sound.

Before long we got to know a lot of our neighbours quite well. Through the wall we had the Ballantynes. Nora Ballantyne was on the staff at Dalneigh and would become my teacher in Primaries 6 and 7, although they had by then moved to Fairfield Road.

On the other side there were the Bells who had a number of children, including Marion who was my age and we played together a lot early on. Across the road at number 13, through the wall from the Crooks, were a rather eccentric couple, the Raches. Ernst Rache was German although he spoke very little of the language. Indeed, so soon after the war, he may well have wanted to keep his Teutonic roots as unobtrusive as possible and he went under the Anglicised form of Ernest.

His devoted wife Alice frequently referred to him as "Dear Ernest" and indeed in private at home that was what we, somewhat patronisingly, also dubbed him. They owned quite a large car although it was also rather aged to the extent of not having a heater. As a result, Dear Ernest would chivalrously escort Alice out to the vehicle, open the door, duly install her inside and wrap a travelling rug carefully around her before closing her in and driving away. The whole process then went into reverse on their return. Meanwhile no one could quite understand why Alice never took her Christmas decorations down until around March.

At times, another neighbour, whom I shall call Mrs *****, was at the talk of the street. It took a few years for my mother to be able to explain this to me, but Mrs *****, a widow, had an occasional boarder. This gentleman was a commercial traveller called Mr. Lovie and perhaps suffice it to say he was Lovie by nature as well as by name. Whether or not this professional itinerant had similar arrangements in other towns he visited, we never found out, but this one became common knowledge in our street. And by the moral standards of the time, it scandalised some.

There was a rather sad end to that tale because Mr Lovie apparently died quite suddenly at some other location. However, the nature of the liaison meant that few if any outwith St Andrew Drive knew anything about it. Neither, therefore, was anyone else aware of Mrs *****, never mind the need for her to be told. It eventually emerged that she spent some time simply not knowing why he had suddenly disappeared from her existence.

Three doors down from us at number 8 were the

MacPhersons. Fiona MacPherson was one of five kids from St Andrew Drive, and indeed all from the same side of the street, who were in my class at school. As it happened all five also went on to the Academy after the promotion exam. Later on, the MacPhersons left and the McBeys made the short move from St Fergus Drive into that house. Well over 50 years later, Mrs McBey still lived there and so, across the road, did Mrs Jessiman who was one of the original residents.

Although some families migrated to private estates, others therefore had very long stays indeed in their council houses. A certain number just stuck where they were for decades, often buying their dwellings after Margaret Thatcher made this possible in the 1980s. Sometimes the next generation would take over the same house, as happened next door to us. The Bells moved out during the 60s and were replaced by Jack and Betty Irvine, Jack being the Mine Host at the Citadel Bar. Half a century later, their daughter was still in the same house.

Our telephone wasn't quite a novelty since 70, Kenneth Street had had one with a three digit number in that pre-Subscriber Trunk Dialling era. Very soon after our move to Dalneigh, just as STD was coming in, we also got the phone there with a five digit number - 30716 - to fit into the new system. When even more capacity was required later, this became 230716 and, outwith large cities, six digit numbers remain to this day. To start with we had to have a party line, shared with Mrs Green along the road, and a completely private conversation was never guaranteed for anyone with such an arrangement. Dalneigh positively bristled with telephone poles and dripped with wires as more and more lines were installed.

Phones in Inverness had come a long way since their introduction in the 1870s. Legal firm MacAndrew and Jenkins had the number Inverness 1 while the Courier was Inverness 59 and Stratton Dairy 754. By the 1960s, the addition of 3s and 0s for STD converted these to 33001, 33059 and 33754.

Up until the early 60s, access to shops was an ongoing problem for much of Dalneigh. The four in Laurel Avenue were a long way away from several streets, including St Andrew Drive, and some found it easier to go to Bruce Avenue.

There was partial relief from the various vans which plied their trade round the streets and these often did a roaring trade. The van would stop in a street and sound its horn or ring a bell, bringing out a queue of housewives.

Bobby MacKay brought a wide range of butchery products, including his superb steak and kidney pies with a tantalising touch of spice in them. Jocky Lawson's grocery van was packed to the rafters although this wasn't a universally popular service. Jocky himself was fine but the problem was the snippy Mrs Lawson who usually accompanied him. Here we had the Basil Fawlty of grocery long before John Cleese, and not a few took great exception to receiving Mrs Lawson's service, decidedly without a smile.

Because of the trek to Alicky Fraser in Laurel Avenue, Lawson's van pretty well still had the monopoly so initially didn't suffer much loss of trade. But when the Lawsons moved instead to one of the new shops at the end of St Andrew Drive, there was competition across the road when Jimmy Christison opened in the other one and was noticeably busier.

There were also a couple of fish vans while Harry Barclay's wagon, often on a Saturday afternoon, would bring pink or blue paraffin. This was the essential fuel for the myriad heaters which supplemented coal fires in keeping homes warm before central heating

Early morning milk deliveries came from rival companies Farmers' Dairy in green livery or Stratton in orange. Electric floats had overwhelmingly replaced horse drawn wagons and Dalneigh's long serving Ecky Duncan was probably the last to use horsepower. These electric motors may not have disturbed sleeping residents at 5am but bottles, especially rattling empties, in their metal crates most certainly did.

In the dead of winter, the milk had often frozen by the time it was collected from the front step. The resulting expansion raised a white column above the mouth of the pint bottle, with the aluminum top sitting on it. In the summer the problem was birds pecking through these tops and means had to be devised to protect them. Skimmed and semi-skimmed milk were little more than a glint in a progressive dietitian's eye and the top two inches of each bottle had just that slightly darker colour where the cream formed an upper layer. You could shake it to mix milk and cream, but my greatest joy of a morning was cornflakes and sugar with "the top of the bottle" on them.

The most popular arrival, though, was the ice cream van - or on some occasions a chap with a bike and a big cold box on the front. One or two of the Italians had vans but probably the most famous was Pagliari's quaint little pale blue, bubble shaped one that went right round the town. You always knew when it was Pagliari's van because of the very distinct tune it played - the Harry Lime theme from the Orson Welles film The Third Man. This was always guaranteed to bring young and old alike out of their houses.

Who sold the best ice cream in Inverness has been a matter of debate for decades. Some said it was Pagliari's, others opted for the Ness Cafe or Salvadori's or one or the other Italians. But strangely, one very strong favourite wasn't Italian at all. Stratton Dairy had a shop opposite the Old High

The Ness Cafe - one of many long lost Italian favourites.

Church in Church Street, and the ice cream produced there was very highly rated indeed. There was also the odd fish and chip van around the town, including one which did a roaring trade on a roundabout down the Ferry.

Entertainment for kids was still pretty primitive in the late 1950s. Apart from basic toys and well established comics, there really wasn't much. We didn't acquire a TV until 1959, leaving us only our brown and cream radio with its metal grill. About the size of a lemonade crate, it was packed full of pretty ancient technology, notably thermionic valves for amplifying the signal. Although the transistor had been invented a few years previously, it was barely in general use and even that has long since been replaced by integrated circuits.

A thermionic valve was an evacuated glass envelope, perhaps the size of a small medicine bottle, whose circuitry allowed electrons to travel in one direction only, but in doing so it had the ability to amplify current and hence the radio signal. These took several seconds to heat up and the radio could not work until after that induction period. There were several valves in a radio set - or "wireless" as many still called them - so it could get very warm indeed.

Tuning was through a variable capacitor, altered by turning a knob round and round and the same mechanism swept a pointer across an illuminated glass screen with exotic names on it like Hilversum, Allouis, Helsinki and Sottens.

Much less exotic was the variety of BBC stations available from the UK. The Home Service carried mainly news, documentaries, drama and other speech based transmissions. Its cornerstone was "Today", the morning news, and as "The Today Programme", that remans the flagship of Radio 4, which the Home Service became in 1967. Another morning standard was the religious feature "Lift Up Your Hearts" while politics received coverage from "Yesterday In Parliament" at an early hour and

"Today In Parliament" in the evening. Live broadcasting of the Commons and Lords was still a long way away. There was also a significant input from Scotland.

Then there was the Light Programme where my personal highlight was Listen with Mother with its stories and nursery rhymes, often presented by Daphne Oxenford. One of its theme tunes, the Berceuse from Gabriel Faure's Dolly Suite, was probably the first piece of classical music I ever heard. And then there was the story - "Are you sitting comfortably? Then I'll begin."

However my days of regular listening to this were already over since it was broadcast at 1:45, so I could only catch it during school holidays. Its title was also a reflection of the times, predicated on the assumption that most mothers did not work.

The Saturday morning highlight was Uncle Mac's Children's Favourites, presented by Derek McCulloch. This delighted youngsters across the country with its record requests, some of which became synonymous with the programme. Danny Kaye's "Ugly Duckling", the Goons' "Ying Tong Song" and "Little White Bull" with Tommy Steele are only a sample.

The Light Programme's Sunday regular was "Family Favourites", usually either Two Way or Three Way where the home country was linked up with locations where many British forces were still serving such as Cyprus - or Germany where we had BAOR (British Army On The Rhine). It was a request show to unite families with distant members, many still absent on National Service, and addresses were normally quoted as their numbered BFPO (British Forces Post Office). This would frequently feature contemporary favourites such as "Catch A Falling

Star" or "Memories Are Made Of This" or Jim Reeves' perennial weepy "Scarlet Ribbons" - or indeed something from the burgeoning rock and roll repertoire.

The Home Service became Radio 2 in BBC Radio's 1967 reorganisation while the unimaginatively named Third Programme became Radio 3. Although Radio 3 still broadcasts a blend mainly of classical music and intellectual content, this is now a good deal less po-faced than its 1950s predecessor.

Most transmissions were on AM, also known as Medium Wave, although the Home Service could be found on 1500m Long Wave. There was also a Short Wave but atmospherics were usually pretty horrendous, as they were to some extent on all AM frequencies before VHF/FM appeared. But because MW, SW and LW all bounced off the ionosphere, they had a very long range – hence some of the more exotic names on old radio dials. I used to spend quite a lot of time squealing and whining my way across the wave bands using that capacitor knob.

Throughout my childhood, we as a family had to wait just a little longer than some others for some of the luxuries in life which were then proliferating. Although we eventually got them, we were by no means the first in the street to have a washing machine, a car, a fridge, a TV and so on. My parents had quite an old fashioned attitude to "debt", including Hire Purchase, and their aim was to buy things as far as possible only when they could be owned outright.

This also explained our relatively late departure from Dalneigh to our own house at Holm Mills. They wanted to put down as large a deposit as possible and then the mortgage was paid off well within its term. One exception was when the Encyclopaedia Britannica salesman came calling and the children's version, at considerable cost and possibly by way of other sacrifices, was purchased on the spot.

In retrospect this decision played an enormous role in my development. These twelve red volumes arrived when I was around eight, just when I was developing a thirst for knowledge. And what a thirst that was, partly assuaged and partly intensified by that Children's Britannica. Admittedly within a relatively narrow range in the case of fiction, I did read prodigiously and a volume of the Britannica would often go to bed with me at night. My mother often knew when I had spontaneously dropped off to sleep since she would hear the book hit the floor above and she would go up to switch off my bedside lamp.

This may seem quite "geeky" but it's the way I

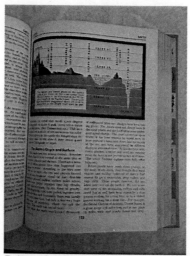

The Children's Britannica was a great source of information.

50

have always been. When I find myself interested in a subject - and I am interested in many - I find an irresistible desire to find out about it. For instance, when I awoke to classical music in my mid teens, I spent much of my time reading about it. I spent hours in Bruce Miller's music shop in the Market reading the backs of record sleeves and classical music became my specialist subject on Mastermind in 1973. When the Inverness football merger came along in 1993, I saw it as a profound event in the social history of Inverness and ended up writing the official account of it for Caley Thistle. And when Covid19 reared its head in 2020, I spent much of the lockdown finding out about this new virus and compiling statistics on its spread and retreat. One other area of particular interest is history and finding out about that is one of many things directly traceable to the Children's Britannica.

That encyclopaedia was soon supplemented by the magazine Look and Learn which ousted Harold Hare as the reading material my dad brought home weekly - along with the Valiant comic after it appeared in 1962. Headlined by Captain Hercules Hurricane and his batman Maggot Malone, The Valiant also had stories about Billy Bunter, Kelly's Eye and Sexton Blake. Most other comics could be caught up on whilst waiting for a haircut at Diggar's.

It was therefore 1959, by which time there were already several large H-shaped aerials attached to other neighbouring chimney pots, before the TV arrived. The option of hiring one had been firmly rejected and a 14 inch KB Queen was eventually purchased. This 405 line set was quite up-market, since my parents did also tend to wait until they could afford a decent version of whatever they were buying.

By modern standards it was, of course, still pretty primitive. Colour TV was still a decade or more away and two of the main features of this black and white model were its horizontal and vertical holds. These were controls which frequently had to be used to prevent the picture from spinning in these directions and there were also controls to regulate black-white contrast. If an "unsuppressed" vehicle, especially a motor bike, went up the street the picture would temporarily degenerate into a blizzard due to radiation from the spark plugs.

Its valves meant that it took several seconds to warm up and when you switched it off, the picture collapsed into a gradually shrinking white dot. It was said that the first TV addicts used to wait until that dot had finally disappeared after they switched off at night. Changing channel wasn't a problem because there was only one channel - The BBC Television Service. Grampian TV and then BBC2 were still some years away and even the single channel ran only until around 11pm, at which point the National Anthem would always be played. Daytime transmissions were broken by Interludes covered by films, most famously The Potter's Wheel, or the Test Card.

Compared with later years, this really didn't leave the BBC with much television airtime to fill in the late 1950s. There were, of course, news bulletins where Richard Baker had become the BBC's first on-screen newsreader. The "Tonight" magazine programme, presented by Cliff Michelmore, was an early evening favourite, with roving reporter Fyfe Robertson whose demeanour and in particular his accent would have dismissed him as a caricature Scotsman - if he hadn't been a real one.

For men (and so it was in these days), Barry Bucknell had a DIY programme while Percy Thrower was the BBC's gardening expert. Meanwhile "women's interests" were covered by the cooking programmes of Fanny and Johnny Cradock, and Tony Hart was a legend in the field of art.

Children had CrackerJack (Hooray!!) with Eamon Andrews, Leslie Crowther and Peter Glaze alongside such icons as Andy Pandy, Bill and Ben the Flowerpot Men... and of course Weed. Then there was drama, where no Sunday night would be complete without my granny's favourite, Dr Finlay's Casebook. Bill Simpson played the eponymous hero, Andrew Cruickshank was Dr Cameron and Barbara Mullen, an American with an awful cod-Highland accent, played Janet the housekeeper.

Well at least I think Dr Finlay won by a short head with my granny, from Dixon of Dock Green (Evening All!) with Jack Warner, then in his mid-60s playing what must have been Britain's oldest copper.

If you didn't want to walk the mile or so from Dalneigh to the town, there was quite a good bus service with a juvenile fare of around 3d. The scheme was well served by the St Valery Avenue route which tended to offer the nearest stops to home, but also Laurel Avenue and a less convenient Dalneigh service. One St Valery bus was, for years, scheduled to arrive outside Dalneigh Primary School at 4pm and as a result the afternoon bell went at 3:55.

Most of the buses were red double deckers, all with their conductresses (or "clippies") whose metallic silver machines spewed out narrow strips of ticket from a roll. These buses offered a route to a world outside the relatively confined limits of the Dalneigh housing scheme from which a young child had limited opportunities to escape.

One clear memory from my earliest time in Dalneigh was the constant metallic "thump, thump, thump" of the steam hammer which drove the piles of the new Ness Bridge into the river bed, placing the date at around 1960.

The belated arrival of this bridge is part of a lengthy tale which begins in 1939 as war clouds began to gather irrevocably. The iconic 225 foot suspension bridge, which had sufficed since its opening in 1855, was said to be reaching the end of its lifetime as vehicles became both more numerous and heavier. A single tower and arch at its Bridge Street end limited traffic flow across this unique, asymmetric structure and traffic lights were installed. In 1939 it was scheduled for replacement and a temporary bridge with trademark white wooden slats on its sides was built about 50 yards upstream. Then the war broke out and everything stopped, but with the temporary structure now carrying traffic from the town centre and the original in the opposite direction.

If there had been doubts about the old bridge's ability to carry heavier vehicles, these would have been dispelled by the tanks which flowed through the town for the duration of hostilities. The confidence derived from this, amid post-war austerity, may have contributed to delaying its replacement until 1959. At that point, the old bridge was demolished, leaving the temporary one as the sole crossing until the new one as complete.

That was constructed between 1959 and 1961 by Duncan Logan and Company of Muir of Ord. This firm was fronted by the charismatic Willie Logan and took on a vast number of contracts, including the Tay Bridge which opened in 1966. However 1966 also saw Willie Logan's death when his private plane crashed into Craig Dunain hill near Inverness. Although the construction company is no longer, his name still lives on in the airline Loganair which he also founded.

Willie Logan's house, Parklea on Kinnairdie Brae in Dingwall, was an imposing local landmark with a massive garden stretching down to what used to be the main A9. It was full of the latest technological gadgets and I once found myself inside it since my aunt and uncle, having moved from Invergordon, became his neighbours across the road - albeit in an altogether less imposing dwelling. During my latter primary school years, when family holidays were difficult due to my ageing grandmother, I was often despatched on the train to Dingwall for a few days and my visit to Parklea was during one of these stays.

The departure of the suspension bridge fostered two enduring traits among some Invernessians. Some, including myself, continue sixty years on to refer to its replacement as "The New Bridge". However I do not subscribe to the other trait which is the belief that the suspension bridge was such a landmark that it should have been left in place. Traffic volumes have long since increased well beyond the capacity of the old structure with its pinch point arch.

The bridge replacement did also catalyse a series of architectural events. Some of these were necessary but many of the others are instances of environmental vandalism for which Inverness has become notorious.

The buildings on the south side of Bridge Street were certainly well past their best and, with urgent need also to widen the road, these needed to be demolished. However that demolition, was probably more extensive than necessary. The old library, police station and fire station below the castle and the unique Castle Tolmie on the corner of Ness Bank also disappeared very soon after the suspension bridge.

Castle Tolmie, where The Shapla now is, and the tower of the suspension bridge.

Then, into the 1960s, there occurred a series of architectural travesties which continue to blight the Highland Capital - and to an ever-increasing extent, as they also undergo terminal decay.

CHAPTER 3 - BEYOND THE NEST.

From around the age of nine - a lot younger, anyway, than normally permitted now - I was allowed to leave the immediate precincts of the house unsupervised, especially to meet friends. These were modest outings initially, but they steadily became more extensive and ambitious. I had quite a wide range of friends, some of them individual pals, but also a group of five or six classmates - a rogues' gallery which deserves the entire chapter after this one to itself.

One individual chum was Dallas Fraser, a red haired boy who lived at number 29. His dad, Jack, was a telephone engineer and there was an older brother, Jackie, a pupil at the Academy. Some of my earliest releases from the family home were with Dallas, including one with a very unfortunate end.

When we first moved to Dalneigh, a 20 yard wide strip of grass separated St Mungo and St Margaret's Roads, both of which had houses only on one side, facing inwards across that grass. Interrupted only by the short road link between St Andrew Drive and Dalneigh Road, this grass strip ran the entire length of these twin streets. However in the early 60s the Council started building right along it - +mainly single storey houses but also two much needed shops at the split.

When work started, Dallas and I adopted the foundations as a play area. As a building site, modern Health and Safety would require it to be securely fenced off. But at this time there was free access to yards and yards of foundations with parallel wooden beams a few feet apart which it was great fun to run along.

At least that was until Dallas slipped and came down with a clatter - and an enormous spray of blood - on one of the beams. He landed face first and the impact forced his front teeth through his lip, creating the most dreadful mess. He was also slightly concussed so I had to leave him with a couple of passers by and run the couple of hundred yards to his house to get his mother. Dallas ended up with an array of black stitches and a scar.

These shops transformed life in the area and one of them became almost a social hub. Jimmy Christison had come to Inverness from Edinburgh in 1934 as manager of the Maypole Dairy but, well into his 50s, decided to go it alone and took out a lease on the shop on the school side. He made a very smart move in bringing with him two of his Maypole staff, Margaret Miller and Bunty MacKenzie. Along with Mrs Christison and the Christison daughters, they made a very slick and obliging retail team.

You could buy most convenience items from Christison's, apart from newspapers which were probably the saving grace for Jocky Lawson who took the shop opposite. It was strange that two grocer's shops should go into the same new development but Christison's got the lion's share of the trade. That was more than evident looking inside and part of this must have been Mrs Lawson's extreme surliness which was well known from the van. Over in Christison's it was service with a smile and an abundance of groceries, cigarettes, confections and sundry knick knacks.

Behind the main counter sat those traditional jars of sweets - bonbons, acid drops, chocolate nuts and many others - generally selling at around 6d or 9d a quarter. There was also the legendary "Penny

Box", and sometimes also a ha'penny box and a tuppeny box, where eager kids could make their choice of dainties or barley sugar or other confectionery. Another favourite was the frozen Milky Way with an ice lolly stick pushed into its end.

For a while "Flags Of The World" bubble gum was all the rage, I wasn't all that keen on bubble gum but I loved collecting the cards wrapped in the packets. These had a flag on the front and on the back there were snippets of the country's language such as how to say simple things like "Hello", "Goodbye" and "Thanks". These cards really built up my knowledge of the world's flags - or at least as they stood in the early 1960s.

Sometimes I would be sent on my own to Christison's to get one or two "messages" - or not infrequently, for around 4/6d, 20 cigarettes since both my parents were smokers. My father gave up when he had a heart attack in 1973 and my mother not long after. I now instantly notice and recoil from cigarette smoke any time I encounter it but, along with many contemporaries, I was brought up in an almost permanent atmosphere of fag smoke for years. No one really thought twice about it at a time, when much less was known about the health hazards.

What normally made a living room need redecorated was how brown the walls and especially the ceiling had become from cigarette smoke and emissions from the coal fire. This was what kept painters and decorators in regular employment rather than worn wallpaper. Tobacco was also responsible for discolouring everything from car interiors to smokers' fingers – the latter a sickly yellow, although in heavy smokers these would turn dark brown.

I've had a basic dislike of cigarette smoke for as long as I can remember but my mother still wanted to be sure I didn't follow in her footsteps and become a smoker myself. One day, just after she lit up, I asked her what a cigarette tasted like - and she invited me to try hers. That was a very shrewd move indeed because, as she knew would happen, I found the thing absolutely disgusting and a definite dislike became a violent, life-long aversion.

Two of my very earliest friends from Dalneigh remain friends more than 60 years on. I had known Iain Steven, who lived in Lilac Grove, since before school because his parents were from Wick and knew mine. Then one day, just weeks after I started at Dalneigh School, I was walking along St Mungo Road with my mother and Irene Lilley, one of my new classmates, ran down her front path and offered me a grape! All three of us went through Dalneigh and the Royal Academy together before becoming part of a very tight knit group of students, mostly from Inverness, at Edinburgh University. We still hold reunions and get togethers.

However in primary school, boys tended mainly although not entirely to hang about with boys and girls with girls and Irene's best pals were the minister's daughters Sheila and Helen MacIntyre and one of my near neighbours, Fiona MacPherson. There was also Catherine Zajac whose father was a Polish tailor - with an eventful wartime career, it was said. Meanwhile Iain and I usually hung around together, often visiting each other's homes. We were also academic rivals and in the twice yearly tests throughout Dalneigh School, Iain would finish top of the class and I would be second.

We also had a shared inability to play football but we did pursue other more cultural interests such as the popular I-Spy and Ladybird books. We were regular visitors to the Public Library and during these years we had to go no further than a portakabin in King Street. The old library in Castle Wynd had been demolished along with the whole of the south side of Bridge Street and it would take some time for its replacement in Upper Bridge Street to come on stream. At the time, if you over-ran the two week lending period, the fine was a penny per day. If you were lucky enough to have a ten shilling note, or even half a crown, the trick was to proffer that in the hope that they would have no change and let you off.

In particular we were Enid Blyton fans, which may well hold special retrospective fascination for Iain who went on to do a degree in English and teach the subject. Blyton was all the rage in the 50s and 60s and I spent much of my pocket money on her books. A Secret Seven hard back cost 7/6d, as did a volume of the Famous Five, while some of the school stories were starting to come out as Armada paperbacks at 2/6d.

I was fortunate to have an older cousin whose Blyton hand me downs I inherited. These included most of the Adventure series - the Castle, Valley, River, Island etc - where a group of four teenagers contrived at will to assist the British Secret Service right across the UK and Europe in dealing with the most sinister of villains.

My perception of Blyton changed during early adulthood. I loved her books as a kid, got completely absorbed in these frequent bed time alternatives to the Children's Britannica, and read most of them again and again. Then, in my 20s, I happened to come across an Enid Blyton book in the Public Library and started reading it.

I was immediately left stone cold by what had enthralled me a dozen years earlier and it is said that Blyton's books, although a joy to children, have that effect on adults. This also got me evaluating, as an adult, many of the characters and story lines I had loved so much, and I found myself horrified. The penny dropped that Enid Blyton was actually a seriously screwed up woman.

She had a father complex - her fathers are almost always absent, at best distant, or sinister like Uncle Quentin. She was a condescending, class conscious snob - most of the kids in her stories go to boarding school and have an incredibly patronising attitude towards the lower social orders. She was acutely xenophobic - foreigners were always sinister and evil, invariably speaking English with the thickest of accents, while gypsies and fairground people were equally despised and untrustworthy. And there are also occasional Nazi undertones - the "Fuhrer" of the Secret Seven, whose meeting shed had a big "SS" on the door, is a nasty little fascist by the name of Peter and, as in Nazi Germany, women know their place. There was more than met the eye to lashings of ginger beer on Kirrin Island and a jolly good laugh at Constable Goon. And was George from the Famous Five "trans" long before "their" time?

It would still be difficult to overstate the pleasure I got from reading Enid Blyton. This lasted from around age eight to 12 but felt a good deal longer. That also applied to other activities of the latter primary school years like building bonfires, playing with friends, going to the Caley Park and indeed schooldays themselves. It was a small slice of life but in fond retrospect feels like an idyllic eternity.

In 1964, Iain and I undertook a major project, pooling our Meccano sets to build a large model of the Forth Road Bridge which had just been opened. I often wonder where I found the time for all my interests because constructing models from Meccano's red plates, green strips, nuts, bolts wheels etc was another big attraction. Meccano, like Lego, promoted genuine creativity.

The model was assembled over several days in Iain's bedroom. This was possibly accompanied by the sounds of contemporary hits like Millie's "My Boy Lollipop", "Little Children" by Billy J Kramer and the Dakotas or the rapidly emerging Beatles' "Can't Buy Me Love", all on the Dansette record player which the Steven family had acquired. We also tried to mount the bridge's base plates on wheels and take the thing on a half mile journey to my house, but as early as the bottom of Laurel Avenue, the wheels literally came off!

Iain was the proud owner of a telescope and we used to take it with us on expeditions to the foreshore of the Beauly Firth, beyond the harbour and close to where the Kessock Bridge now is. It was a very long walk from Dalneigh, longer even than to Whin Island where we would take large potatoes and some tin foil and cook them on an open fire. It was all very Swallows and Amazons, books which we both got as prizes in Primary 7.

We were also friendly with two of the girls from our class, Elizabeth Campbell and Sandra Stuart. Elizabeth's brother Alec was the proud owner of a bike with smaller wheels than usual which made it easily managed. And in the garages behind my house that was how, aged 10, I belatedly learned the art of two wheeled transport. I was then bought a second hand bike of my own, newly painted red and white. My parents decided not to go overboard on a new machine that I would soon grow out of, and in any case they believed that life's luxuries were better appreciated at the end of a wait.

My other main friend was Tommy Cumming who lived on Bruce Gardens, at its junction with St Valery Avenue. Tommy, the son of a stalwart in the Labour Party and the Methodist Church, local Councillor Jack Cumming, was at least as non-sporty as I was, and this reflected in what we did together.

Tommy was very keen on the theatre and we built our own stage out of cardboard, glue and paint bought from Keith's the stationer. He was also quite musical - the only boy in the class who went to piano lessons and he was teased surprisingly little about it. My parents gave me that same chance and we had a piano on which I spent a fair time picking out tunes by ear. But, fearing a threat to my male street cred, I declined the offer.

Tommy was a very good singer too, and his solo rendition of Nobody's Child could bring an audience to tears. This song gained brief popularity in 1964, probably not because the singer was the obscure Tony Sheridan but because the backing was by The Beatles. This was a year for sad songs and one other was the haunting Terry by Twinkle. But while the lyrics of Nobody's Child were clearly and obviously about a blind, unwanted orphan, those of Terry are a little bit less obvious and it needed a couple of older girls to explain to me that this boy had actually died in a motorcycle crash. Appearing as they did very close together, both songs affected me greatly at the time. I used to feel quite disturbed about the sad scenarios they described and both still give me goose bumps if I ever hear them.

Tommy played a ground breaking and pioneering role within one of Inverness's institutions. The Calumdon Girls' Pipe Band was well known throughout the town and at an early age, Tommy broke the mould by becoming its male drum major. This made him a well-known figure at various events, including The Kilt Is Our Delight shows at the Northern Meeting Park.

Our other shared activity was our Christmas shopping. Again, it feels as if we did this often, but it could only have been two or three times. Woolies was the mecca and for our mothers, aunts and Tommy's older sister it was usually these boxes of toilet accessories like bath cubes and foam. As always, fathers were more difficult but we usually got something, spending perhaps a pound each in total. Then it was the bus home to wrap the presents in the copious quantities of Christmas paper and sellotape we also bought.

For a while I used to hang around with Gordon Corrance whose brother Douglas became an eminent photographer and their father, during the Cold War years, was a prominent member of the Civil Defence. Its sister organisation was the Royal Observer Corps which had its origins in the 1920s when concern was rising about future air raids. It came into its own in World War 2, telephoning reports of approaching "bandits" to Fighter Command during the Battle of Britain. One of my father's work colleagues, Sandy Stewart who lived in the Bruce Gardens electric flats, was a member of the ROC which, by the early 1960s, was primarily concerned with incoming nuclear bombers and missiles.

The single most dangerous episode of the Cold War was the Cuba Missile Crisis of October 1962. There was a terrifying face off for several days between American President John F Kennedy and Soviet leader Nikita Khrushchev, who wanted to base nuclear missiles in Cuba, just over 100 miles from Florida. This was eventually resolved, with American missiles in Turkey as a trade off, but there was a spell when the world held its breath in terror of nuclear annihilation.

I was in Primary 5 then and too young to appreciate just how critical this was. I was aware of stuff on the news but I neither understood what it meant nor noticed inevitable nervousness among adults. My generation grew up in a world which for decades, at the touch of a button, could have self-destructed any day. That must be difficult for younger people to understand.

But as I gradually began to comprehend the destructive power of these weapons and the fragility of the relations between the governments controlling them, it didn't overwhelm me. It just seemed part of life and had been so since the late 1940s. You just blocked out thoughts of it, although I did get occasional waves of anxiety later on. I found the immediate aftermath of the 1979 Soviet invasion of Afghanistan especially worrying, and this crisis continued through the SS20 standoff of the mid 80s until Communism collapsed at the end of the decade. But during my youth, I never found the threat of nuclear war an all-consuming issue.

After the Ballantynes went to Fairfield Road, Bill Jack the Burgh Architect moved in through the wall from us until he designed and built his own quite unique house on Stratherrick Road. Next it was the

MacDonalds. "Smeesh" was a commercial traveller and his wife Nan worked for years in Arnotts. Their daughter Brenda was a drummer in the Calumdon Band and their son Derek was another of my play pals. I still meet them both from time to time around Inverness and it's good to get a blether about Dalneigh with these and other former residents.

The Festive Season was a pretty basic celebration. My dad initially had to work on Christmas morning which as much as anything reflected how, in Scotland, New Year was still the main event. We did eventually aspire to going to the Glenmhor Hotel for Christmas lunch which was a real novelty. Owned by Don Manson, assisted by his son Nicol who eventually took it over, the Glenmhor was welcoming and cosy with a lovely wood fire in the hearth. It was the first hotel I had ever been in and remained a favourite for a long time - including as an underage drinking venue.

Presents were generally rudimentary. You hung out a stocking and really did expect the proceeds to include the proverbial orange and a sixpence. Beano and Dandy annuals were common but budgets were limited. By the age of around ten I was allowed to stay up for New Year, which in St Andrew Drive was quite restrained. After the Andy Stewart Show with Dixie Ingram's dancers and Duncan MacRae's Wee Cock Sparra, a few neighbours, including Ernest Rache with an old fashioned basket containing several bottles, would arrive at our house first. The piano would be opened and songs, including Psalms, would be sung before I was left in the charge of my grandmother and the party would move on to a neighbour's.

Drink played a pretty minimal part in our family

life and my parents' main social activity was to have one or two other couples along for the evening, or a reciprocal visit would be made, sometimes with me in tow. The invariable drill (for the adults!) was one drink - usually whisky or sweet sherry - followed by tea and cakes. There was much conversation and, since many of the men were old comrades, I found out quite a lot about World War 2.

In 1963, my dad finally bought a car. Not long after we went to Dalneigh, he got a ricketty moped - RYH 944 - and soon upgraded that to a scooter before finally taking the plunge with a blue second hand Hillman Minx. We were by no means the first family in the area to get a car, but nor were we the last. This made a big difference to my mother, who didn't drive, and to me since we became a lot less dependent on walking or public transport. My dad had driven during the war but hadn't taken it up again soon enough to exempt him from a test so had to go through the whole process with Mr Veitch.

From the start, my dad used MacKenzie and MacPherson at the top of the Raining Stairs both for repairs and for petrol. Housed in an old stable, the garage was run by Duncan MacKenzie and Alastair MacPherson who gave magnificent, old world personal service. Filling stations still largely weren't self-service so one of them would come out and fill your tank for you. And in complete contrast with digital pump readouts which present the capacity to the nearest 10ml and the cost to the nearest penny, a needle would go round at one revolution to the gallon, with any fractions estimated from where it stopped on filling the tank. Six and three quarter gallons at five and sixpence a gallon.... a decade before the first calculators? (I make that one pound

17 and a penny ha'penny!)

Maybe in the 1960s people felt a greater need for their cars to be garaged at night. Few if any houses in Dalneigh had their own facility and there was a waiting list for Council garages, but eventually a wooden one behind St Valery Avenue became available. This was still a bit of a walk from the house but we then got one of the lock ups just 30 yards from our back gate. My first long trip in that car was to Glasgow - but on the tortuous A82, so for a while I thought all roads were like that!

The early 60s produced a major television breakthrough - a second channel, so we at last had to turn that dial.... between positions 1 and 9. Independent Television came to Britain in 1955 but, as usual, the Highlands were at the back of the queue. In 1961 North of Scotland TV, quickly renamed Grampian, began broadcasting locally from studios in Aberdeen's Queens Cross before extending into the Highlands. As with all ITV franchises, there were some local programmes, some from the network... and of course the complete novelty of adverts!

It was extremely Aberdeen orientated and its early presenters included Douglas Kynoch, Jimmy Spankie and "The Torry Quine" June Imrie. Doric abounded, not least in Bothy Nichts, presented by John Mearns. Here various groups – some verging on Doric caricatures - depicted evening entertainments of previous generations in Aberdeenshire agricultural bothies with various farm servants doing their turn. "Couthy" and "Kailyard" it may have appeared to many Highland viewers, but this was the culture of neighbouring Aberdeenshire. The Ingle Neuk was just as culturally foreign to us in the Highlands but we did have the dubious compensation of the Calum Kennedy show.

I found myself far more interested in Grampian's network programmes. The Saint, starring Roger Moore, had a particular local interest since his car registration – ST1 - was from Inverness. This was the property of ex-Provost Robert Wotherspoon who seemed to have some kind of fixation about being "number one" since he also had Ross shire's JS1 and the telephone number Inverness 1, later 33001, for his solicitors' office. It was said that he had been invited to sell ST1 to The Saint's producers but declined and instead gave them permission to use it in the programme.

The Avengers starred Patrick Macnee whose series of glamorous leading ladies included Honor Blackman as Cathy Gale and Diana Rigg as Emma Peel - in still slightly risque black leather catsuits. American comedy classics abounded. I used to love The Beverly Hillbillies, a tale of oil rich country boys and girls who moved to a Hollywood mansion. I found Lucille Ball hilarious and Phil Silvers as Sergeant Bilko remains timeless.

ITV also had children's semi-historical dramas based round legendary heroes. Robin Hood, with its unmistakable signature tune, starred Richard Greene as Robin and Archie Duncan as Little John, and was probably the best known. However there were also William Tell, Sir Francis Drake, Sir Lancelot and Ivanhoe, all made in the UK in the mid-1950s and continually rebroadcast.

Most memorably of all, on Saturday afternoons ITV had the Wrestling segment of World of Sport. This precursor of WWF was, of course, a complete set up with elaborately choerographed moves and poetic justice often handed out to one or other of many "baddies" on the circuit – especially in the tag matches where rule breaches and outrageous cheating were especially prevalent.

There were showmen like Jackie Pallo, Hungarian favourite Tibor Szacacks and Andy Robin with Herculos the Bear. And then there were the baddies like Steve Logan and "Crybaby" Jim Breaks. Kendo Nagasaki, and the camp Adrian Street added another dimension to this world of Boston crabs, forearm smashes, piledrivers, falls, submissions and knockouts.

The BBC fought back with Hiram Holliday, the American geek who fenced his way to safety with his umbrella, and Harry Worth, the eccentric Englishman who did a wonderful splits on the corner of a shop window. British eccentricity was further compounded by Eric Sykes with Hattie Jacques as his sister, and (Tony) Hancock's Half Hour.

Initially, ITV's adverts were a novelty and many of the jingles really took off. "You'll wonder where they yellow went when you brush your teeth with Pepsodent"..... "Now hands that do dishes can feel soft as your face with mild green Fairy Liquid".... "1001 cleans a big, big carpet for less than half a crown". Early British TV jingles seemed to rely heavily on the American barbers' shop style, but these soon gained their own character. "Go to work on an egg", with the little lion stamp became iconic. However it didn't take long for the novelty of commercials to wear off and they soon became a regular inconvenience.

The other TV breakthrough of the period was Telstar. Launched in 1962, this satellite provided the first live transatlantic transmissions. It also inspired a memorable instrumental single of that name by The Tornados whose hits, along with those of the Shadows, epitomised much of pop music in the early 60s – those dying days of performers with short hair and a more conventional demeanour.

A cinema visit to the Playhouse or the La Scala would give you the main event such as Ben Hur, Dr. No or Mary Poppins, but you went for the whole afternoon or evening. Highland Omnibuses even timed their final services for around 1045 to coincide with the end of "the pictures". Along with the main film there was a low budget "B" movie, often in black and white. So was Pathe News; introduced by a cockerel crowing this was an established source of information until television took over. It was as integral a part of any trip to the cinema as the National Anthem at the end of the performance, which by the 60s had started to prompt a spontaneous stampede for the door.

Pathe News had a unique style and ambience. To a busy background, very much in the 1950s light music style, a narrator would jovially relate the story in the clipped, upper crust, classically "British" broadcasting tones of the mid 20th century. One of the best known narrators was Bob Danvers Walker whose distinctive voice was later heard on Michel Miles' "Take Your Pick", a rival and ITV stablemate of Hughie Green's "Double Your Money".

It was at this time that I acquired my first transistor radio. The transistor component was slightly smaller than a cigarette butt with three protruding wires, and rapidly replaced thermionic valves so radios were becoming much smaller. My first "tranny", which could fit in a pocket and switched on instantly, had a leather case and earplug and cost something like £2-19-6. Although pirate radio stations were all the rage, the fully legitimate Radio Luxemburg on 208 metres medium wave was the hot favourite. In particular Luxemburg had a Sunday night UK Top 20 programme and I was one of many surreptitious young listeners who retreated under their bedclothes to catch The Hollies, The Shadows or The Animals.

The 1960s were a decade of great change but life was still pretty uncomplicated. Its highlights tended to be a visit to the football or the cinema or the swimming pool. Pocket money was limited - mine started at a shilling and took a couple of years to rise to half a crown - but you could actually buy quite a lot with that. A number of things seemed to cost around sixpence. These included a bar of chocolate - typically Dairy Milk or Fry's Cream or Five Boys - a bag of chips and a comic.

Once a year, I really found myself in the money. My father had an aunt who was maid to a Lady Roundway in a posh apartment overlooking Hyde Park in London. "Auntie Ciss", who worked into her 80s until "Milady" died, would take the train to Inverness and stay with us for a few nights in the summer and because she lived in London with an aristocrat, I always thought she was terribly, terribly posh. When she eventually died at the age of 105, we discovered that she was indeed reasonably well off for her quite humble status. It turned out that she kept a fair stash of cash in her chest of drawers - while her friend sent her assets to relations in Abriachan in paper parcels!

For my birthday, Auntie Ciss would always send me a crisp Bank of England pound note which was like winning the lottery. Within days, I would be down town on a major shopping spree. That usually included an Airfix model - perhaps the Bismarck or HMS Hood or a Lancaster bomber - or Lego bricks from MacLeay's in Church Street. Woolies' pick and mix was bled dry before the short trip along High Street to MacKay's book shop, which also had a lending library.

Apart from the Meccano set, my only other sophisticated toys were an electronics kit and a Chemistry Set. The electronics arrived one Christmas in a box packed with transistors, resistors, coils and wiring. The idea was to make your own radio, flashing light, burglar alarm etc, but I was a bit too young for this and didn't get the full benefit.

I probably got far more in that department out of a Ladybird book called "Magnets Bulbs and Batteries" with its experiments in simple current electricity using stuff you could buy in the shops. I used to trawl through the electrical department on Woolies' upper floor buying 3 Volt bulbs, bulb holders, yards of insulated wire and a pile of Ever Ready batteries, including chunky 4.5 volt bell batteries, and this kept me occupied for hours. Series and parallel lighting circuits, electromagnets, primitive DC electric motors even. With this book, they could all be made out of stuff from Woolies.

Given how much time I later spent showing children how to work safely in a scientific environment, I look back on with horror on the Chemistry Set. The 1960s Chemistry Set was meant to be educational and to an extent was, but it was also a potential death trap.

Its chemicals were just the start. You heated Sodium Thiosulphate to get highly poisonous Hydrogen Sulphide gas, which also stank the house out with its eggy aroma. The ability of Potassium Permanganate to stain just about anything was only the start of its difficulties. This is also a very ready source of oxygen, creating a significant fire risk - especially if you heated it with the Sulphur to produce the horrible, poisonous, choking gas Sulphur Dioxide and a very hot flame.

Even warming Ammonium Carbonate in a dangerously wafer thin glass test tube filled the place with choking Ammonia, and all of that could be done with the set's simple meths burner. My parents drew the line at my using the bunsen since, apart from a severe fire risk, it had to be hooked up to the cooker which ran on coal gas with its high content of lethally poisonous carbon monoxide. I never experienced worse than a few stinks and one minor conflagration, but other chemistry set users were less fortunate. And I can't attribute to it any of my later inspiration to go on to study Chemistry.

As good a Chemistry experiment as any was the popular drink Creamola Foam which bubbled up furiously when you added water to the coloured powder. This was a simple case of citric acid reacting with sodium bicarbonate, when both dissolved and kids were mad for the stuff. Sherbet, bought in pale yellow tubes with liquorice straws sticking out of them, worked in exactly the same way, but using saliva.

Time was also spent on my dad's Torpedo brand typewriter which, despite its considerable weight, he carried all the way home from Germany in 1946. He needed to have some of the keys altered to meet the UK format and it really wasn't unlike a traditional black Imperial. Although it would be another two decades before I mastered two finger typing, I did get the basics here such as disentangling stuck together keys, using carbon paper and loading a ribbon. Keys striking a solid surface are, of course, noisy but this was nothing compared with what I encountered on walking into a "typeen" class in the late 70s where 20 girls were simultaneously hammering out letters.

For my first holiday, my granny was dispatched for a break with my aunt and uncle in Dingwall and we took the steam train to Glasgow. My mother's other sister and her husband lived near Paisley and we stayed with them. It was intriguing to sit in a compartment built for six and watch swathes of smoke and steam billow past the window while the engine rhythmically laboured up the Slochd or Drumochter. Apart from the steam train, I also got a ride in an equally moribund green and cream Glasgow tram.

In 1963 my mum stayed at home to look after my granny and my dad took me to Butlins in Ayr. The journey to Glasgow was my first flight and we stayed in a hotel there on the Friday night before getting the train to Ayr. This would have been the second week in July because in the morning I heard from our room what sounded like a collection of tin whistles and drums passing along the street outside. I remember my dad's look of horror when I asked to go out to watch. In my youthful Invernessian innocence and naivety, I had no idea at all of what he was painfully aware could involve punch ups, bottle throwing and loudly expressed views about depriving His Holiness of his virginity.

Sometimes the circus - Billy Smart's or Bertram Mills' - would come to Inverness and set up its big top at the Bught after a high profile parade of elephants, clowns and acrobats through the town centre. Other times it was what Inverness called "the shows" but different places dubbed "the fair", "the sideshows" or in Nairn, where they still arrive to coincide with the Highland Games before heading for Inverness, "the showies". The Bught Park was the usual venue and once again 6d was the standard price for the Waltzers, Dodgems or shooting gallery - inevitably using air rifles with suspiciously sawn down sights.

The Bught was even more crucial then than it is now as Inverness's sporting centre, mainly because there were so few alternatives. Surrounded by a wooden stake fence, the inner Bught Stadium housed mainly shinty, but also the Inverness Highland Games and the inter school sports. The outer Bught met most of the football needs of local amateur or welfare sides as well as youth organisations such as the Boys' Brigade, so demand for changing rooms was heavy.

Sometimes the stables at Bught House had to be pressed into service and changing there could be a cold and miserable experience. Both house and stables were demolished later in the 60s and a new ice rink opened at the edge of the park.

Nearer home, Dalneigh got a new play facility, a circular memorial pavilion in the field between the school and the canal which turned out to be a white elephant. There were benches all around the high ceilinged "pavvy" but it never seemed to be used all that much in my time, although the swings, see saw and roundabout outside were a lot busier. It was also frequently vandalised but the play park was very popular.

As the 60s progressed, traffic levels in Inverness

increased so "the new bridge" (as some still call it) had arrived not a moment too soon. The Temporary Bridge was gone, the river bank restored and, apart from the Black Bridge, in an era of increasing car ownership, this sleek new structure now carried pretty well all of the town's burgeoning through traffic. It also solved the small problem of the suspension bridge not having been perfectly aligned with Bridge Street. The new structure was tweaked just that little bit to give a perfectly straight axis.

However the bridge was just the start of a town centre building boom which would last for a decade. Most of Inverness's many architectural eyesores were imposed and inflicted on it in the 1960s and the much more aesthetically pleasing starting point of this environmental vandalism was that new bridge which opened in 1961.

But at least the bridge eased the traffic problem in a town where pairs of trunk roads joined on its east and west sides, and almost the only link between them was through the town centre. The town's three sets of traffic lights at Kenneth Street, the Steeple and Inglis Street were then all along this linking section. Few Invernessians can now remember when Old Edinburgh Road was two way between Castle Street and Southside Road and the creation of road extensions in the Longman as it expanded past Burnett's Bakery to accommodate the likes of J. Arthur Dixon's postcard factory and Inverness Technical College.

The 1961 census recorded Inverness's population as 29,774 but during the next decade, that would grow by almost 20%, one of the biggest increases in the Royal Burgh's history.

CHAPTER 4 – DALNEIGH BOYS.

Apart from my individual friends already described, there was also a group of us who went right through Dalneigh School in the same class. We did a great deal together, mainly sporting activities and general "hanging about", and although we were hardly what anyone might call evil, sometimes we weren't angels either.

There was "Beys" - Brian McBey who lived initially in St Fergus before moving to St Andrew. Since he was the best at football and sport in general, social psychology dictated that Beys was the accepted leader of the group. Then there was "Kavvies" - Brian Kavanagh from 74, St Valery Avenue which looked right down St Andrew. His dad Paddy, an Irishman and a right character with it, worked for the railway. Physically, Kavvies was the smallest of the group but he more than compensated for that with his liveliness and assertiveness. Our base was often the wasteland behind his house, which was hence known as "The Back O' Kavvies'", where we spent countless hours on various activities, both legitimate and occasionally nefarious. "Der" (Derek Barclay) lived a few doors along from Kavvies while "Brems" (Brian Bremner) had a bit further to travel from Caledonian Road, as did Roddy Williamson (known just as "Roddy") from St John's Avenue.

A few others would also join in occasionally, notably "Frasers" (Dallas Fraser), and George Polworth ("Pols") who had contracted a mild form of polio as a young child which left him with a withered lower leg supported by a caliper. This did not deter him from participating to the full and Pols was an extremely popular and fully accepted member of the group. Then there was "Banns" - that was me by the way.

Sometimes we would be accompanied by an honorary member of our group, Beys' dog Penny, who was one of very few canines in whose company I have ever felt completely comfortable. Another was the Rev MacIntyre's spaniel, an extremely mild mannered companion when I would crawl through the hedge between our gardens to play with the MacIntyre children and climb their trees. Penny was a black and white gem almost of the husky variety with very sharp features, equally sharp intelligence and an adorable nature.

Our group would also sometimes include two younger boys from outwith our class group. Gordon and Andrew Smith lived in the last house before the St Valery flats. Their father ran an electrician's shop in the market and their much younger sister became the well known novelist Ali Smith. The Smiths completed a trio of families in a line of just a dozen houses in St Valery Avenue which all had girls as late additions in the early 60s. The Barclays had twins and the Kavanaghs a much younger daughter.

A great deal of time was spent at The Back O' Kavvies' whose features were so diverse that it was almost a theme park. Immediately next to the "Electric Flats" - one of three blocks in Dalneigh powered entirely by electricity - there was an extensive area of undergrowth packed with bushes and narrow winding paths created by previous generations of local kids. That abutted on one side a large cleared area of grass which never seemed to get cut but still never became impossibly long. On another side there were garages, wooden this time with sloping roofs, and all of this bordered the steeply sloping canal banks.

"The Back O' Kavvies'" in 2021. The goal posts were mere jackets in the baby boomer era.

That grass area was our football pitch where jackets would go down for goals, leading to endless arguments about whether a shot resulted in a goal or a miss. These were often resolved by the compromise of a "post". Here the ball was judged to have gone over the jacket, that very near miss coming as minor consolation for the goal not being allowed.

Teams were picked by alternating selections between the captains, often Beys, and Brems who was another very good player, and indeed both progressed as far as the Highland League. As they descended the pecking order, I experienced no suspense because it was inevitable that I would be last. In hindsight I'm maybe surprised that I was accepted at all by this collection of boys since they were all so much better than I was at almost all physical activity. I was REALLY bad but acceptance was never an issue.

I'm also sure it wasn't because we often played with my ball. My great aunt Ciss, the one who used to send me pound notes, also bought me a real size 5 football, which wasn't that common outside clubs. It was one of these really traditional brown leather jobs with a rubber bladder inserted into the casing through a narrow slit pulled tight using a lace after inflation with a bicycle pump.

Lovingly, I rubbed that ball down every week with dubbin, a waxy compound used to keep leather objects soft and waterproof, but it still got absorbent again and sometimes soaked up enough water to make it almost unkickable. It's perhaps unsurprising that, many decades later, brick like objects like these should be associated with dementia among men who headed them for a living for years on end.

Games frequently lasted much longer than the regulation 90 minutes. They often ended in a dispute over whether the score was 23-18 or 24-17 - or when everyone was completely exhausted. Anyone looking for proof that Baby Boomers were a lot fitter than modern youth need go no further than games like these. In the summer, football was sometimes sidelined in favour of cricket where my frequency of ducks was staggering.

My uselessness at sport in primary school was probably down to two things. I was hopeless at running, although this constraint suddenly disappeared at around 13 with life changing consequences. And I just had no ball skills at all, a lifelong affliction, and the reason took several decades to be fully understood. I was into my 50s and reporting on football matches live on radio and television before the penny eventually dropped. The connection between my eyes and my brain is extremely slow and inefficient.

My abysmal football skills in primary school were probably the first indication, but I never linked this to a very poor eye for a ball. I still didn't tumble to it a few years later when I found that the one ball game I wasn't bad at was rugby, as long as someone just put the thing into my hands.

It also took a long time to link my poor ball skills with, for instance, great difficulty counting series of identical objects such as iron railings. And while I have a pretty good musical ear and quickly picked up the theory, I found myself totally unable to read music at any meaningful speed so had to rely on learning parts. Black dots on a grid of lines and spaces became completely scrambled.

On the Top Of The Form quiz I knew I wasn't quite as fast at answering picture questions as those involving speech or music, although in practice my response to sound, such as identifying music, is very fast indeed. In English classes, I was hopeless at reading out loud so was inevitably cast as "Enter a Messenger", although self-consciousness may also have been a factor. And ever since I went into sports broadcasting, reading from a script, especially at my quite rapid rate of delivery, has always needed full concentration.

It eventually dawned after several years of live broadcasting from Caley Thistle and Ross County football matches - ironically incongruous as that may be, given my early football background! Reporting on these games was always very hard work with a constant danger of seeing something happen but not having a clear picture of it. In practice I made very few mistakes, but the effort to achieve that was sometimes exhausting.

So it wasn't until the early 2000s that it gradually dawned that I have a very limited ability to process visual stimuli. But at last here was an explanation for a lot of things, starting with always being the last boy picked at football at the Back O' Kavvies'.

World War 2 had been over for less than 20 years and live bullets were even found about the place from time to time. There was still an acute awareness of the war - even among the generation born shortly after it. I was perhaps a little more tuned into it than my cotemporaries because I was one of a minority among my group of friends whose father had done wartime service. Aged 33 when I was born, my dad was a bit older than those of my friends, so served for the entire duration, and I also grew up meeting many of his army pals.

Awareness of that conflict also influenced how we spent our spare time. Often the Back O' Kavvies', would be transformed into a battlefield and we would "play at war", which seems an incongruous description. Just as Waterloo was allegedly won on the playing fields of Eton, World War 2 was well and truly re-enacted in the early 60s at the Back O' Kavvies'. That undergrowth and the garages were spontaneously transformed into the deserts of North Africa, the jungles of Burma or the bocage of Normandy. Sides were picked as for football and it was usually British against Germans, or occasionally Japanese. The Americans didn't seem to figure.

Each youthful soldier had a free choice of armaments from his imaginary arsenal and off we went to track down and annihilate our opponents. Those who had chosen machine guns (the most popular option) would discharge them by way of rapidly repeating staccato bursts of air from near the back of the throat. Rifles, on the other hand, featured a more strangulated, guttural outburst from around the molars. Hand grenades, meanwhile, detonated by way of an expulsion of air across the tongue and through vibrating lips.

And as with disputed goals, games of war were frequently punctuated by shrill exclamations of "You're dead!!" countered by "No I'm not!!" from urchins covered in sticky willows. The military equivalent of a "post" to resolve a disputed goal was the victim only being declared "wounded", although his future value to his side was then decidedly unclear.

World War 2 was also revisited through Commando comics and other less popular or iconic rival brands like War Picture Library. Selling at around a shilling, these were greatly prized and often exchanged among friends. Kavvies had a wooden box in his bedroom stuffed with them.

Commando comics gave a vivid insight into land, sea and air battles and, despite some pretty improbable story lines, were largely true to history. They were also thoroughly British. Unlike in Hollywood films, you would never see a John Wayne character under the Stars and Stripes simultaneously and single handedly liberating both Western Europe and the entire Pacific.

But maybe they were just a bit too British, especially in their jingoism and racial stereotyping. Most of these publications featured honest, square jawed British soldiery justly prevailing over the nasty, untrustworthy Teutons and the creepy Nipponese.

Commandos also revealed just how limited was the vocabulary of the Third Reich, amounting to little more than "Achtung Englander".... "Gott in Himmel"...."Achtung Schpitfeuer!" and the all-pervasive "Schweinhund!!" And, whether Waffen SS or Panzergrenadier, the forces of Nazism always expired with a terminal cry of "Aaaarggh!". Meanwhile the might of the Rising Sun was less articulate still, with little more to say than "Banzaiii!" and references to "Blittish Johnee", whilst departing life with a blood curdling "Aiiieeee!"

Because the weapons in our games of war were overwhelmingly vocal, there was no place for the humble cap gun, although every boy had one and frequently used it for playing Cowboys and Indians. These replica Colt 45s, and other models, had an internal mechanism into which you could load a roll of 100 caps which were dots of an explosive mixture on a strip of paper. As the hammer came down on the dots, the mixture would detonate with a sharp crack and a unique smell. The guns had a repeating action so shot after shot could be loosed off and you could also make a cap explode by dragging your thumb nail across it. Replica firearms have long since disappeared from Christmas and any other present lists.

The Back o' Kavvies' was also the venue for a major annual celebration. It fell to our group of friends to build a huge Guy Fawkes bonfire there, which was enjoyed by the entire neighbourhood. Not for the first time this is something we seemed to do again and again but it was probably just twice, 1963 and 1964 - perhaps 1962 as well.

This mammoth and eagerly anticipated

construction project began perhaps about two weeks before Bonfire Night. Branches, old planks, bushes, roofing felt and, on the night itself, old newspapers were all pressed into service. We enlisted anything combustible that could be scavenged from the waste ground or from neighbours who were often very glad to unload their junk on the request "Anyheen furtha bonefire?". It was all accumulated with great diligence and the pyramid grew and grew in order to burn itself out pretty well within an hour or two. Football was temporarily abandoned as every effort was focused on this bonfire, although the Guy was usually a pretty rudimentary afterthought.

Our constant worry was that outsiders - with particular concern about "boys from the Ferry" - would creep in under cover of darkness and ruin the whole thing by prematurely setting it alight. "Guarding the bonfire" therefore became a regular task during the latter stages. This involved a group of us gathering in the field and lighting another small fire near the big one - partly to keep us warm, partly to warn off any intruders, but mainly, I suspect, to dispel our fear of the pitch dark.

Of many things we were allowed to do at that age back then, but certainly wouldn't now, hanging about on wasteland on a pitch dark evening must be pretty high on the list. Anything could have happened, but parents seemed not to turn much of a hair, probably because levels of risk were perceived to be much lower. The worst that happened to me was a drip of molten tar from burning felt landing on the back of my left hand. This created a small but deep burn, the 55 year old legacy of which I am currently surveying as I write.

On the night itself, everyone from all around

arrived with their fireworks... or at least fireworks that hadn't already been let off by over-impatient owners. If any childhood memory still sends shivers up my back it's the lack of safety with fireworks, and not just penny bangers. Catherine Wheels, Roman Candles, Jumping Jacks, rockets and many more highly dangerous pyrotechnics were all easily purchased by unsupervised primary school children from various shops. My particular favourite was Toyland on Drummond Street where the Conservative Party constituency office now is.

I must admit that I had something of a fascination with fireworks, which during these weeks accounted for a lot of my pocket money. I usually preferred to choose my own individual items for something between 3d and a shilling each rather than accept the unknowns of a Brocks' or Astra box for half crown or five bob.

The traditional instruction was "Light the blue touch paper and stand well clear" which was quite a minimal safety guide. Then there was always the temptation to break some open to make massive and highly dangerous "genies", far bigger than you would get from a penny banger. And where did I keep these explosives? In a box in the cupboard under the stairs of a wooden Swedish house! It was what everybody just did without a thought.

Our November 5th fireworks display was entirely spontaneous and totally unregulated. Someone suddenly lit a newspaper and threw it into the fire to get the show on the road, opening the floodgates for a massive free for all. People just let off their own personal explosives where and when they wanted. It was complete mayhem for almost an hour and what a miracle it was that no one was ever hurt, although local pets must have been terrified by the din.

Jumping Jacks whizzed erratically about the packed throng while rockets soared up at all angles and sometimes a firework would topple over just as it was ready to spew out pyrotechnic flares. Then, with the smoke of fireworks and the bonfire still in our nostrils and stinking out our clothes, we would head for home, leaving embers which would still be emitting a gentle warmth the following afternoon.

Five days before Guy Fawkes we would briefly abandon bonfire building in order to celebrate Halloween. Until I was about nine, my parents took me round neighbours to sing a terrible song or recite an awful poem in return for what were quite rich pickings. You could easily end the night with a vast stash of peanuts, apples, oranges and sweets and a fair sum in cash. Later on we were allowed to go out unsupervised in groups - pirates, ghosts, cartoon characters, comic heroes - in pursuit of these substantial riches. Costumes, though, were largely obtained from parents' and grandparents' wardrobes - the latter often smelling of mothballs. It would be some time before shops started selling bespoke Halloween garb.

Occasionally, and especially on a hot summer day, we would resort to water fights. Sometimes a hose would be deployed, while other battles would just involve basins from someone's kitchen (which could get left with a very wet floor), but the most common medium for these water fights was very simple indeed. The advert said "It's so easy with Squezy" and that also included soaking your pal.

In the 60s, Squezy was at least as well known as Fairy Liquid when it came to washing up liquids in soft plastic bottles. And when these were finished, kids were always more than happy to take them off their mothers' hands. A full Squezy bottle compressed tightly could project a spout of water several yards which made it a formidable weapon in these encounters.

Other entertainments included "kerbie" where bouncing a football off the far kerb on the wide part of St Andrew Drive was a particular challenge. "Conkers" involved getting a parent to bore a hole in a chestnut (preferably a "kinger") with a hot needle so you could pass the string through before knotting it. Meanwhile marbles (known locally as "derbs") also had their popular season, with "steelies" or "steelucks" especially prized – particularly if one happened to be a large ball bearing. Then there was "skeetchie" or hopscotch where you chalked the numbered outline in the road or pavement and tested your agility by hopping through the squares. "One, two, three Victoria" involved the person who was "it" turning away while reciting that line and quickly turning back to catch any members of an advancing line still moving.

Returning to sport, once or twice our group did hold cycle races round Dalneigh. Going hell for leather round suburban streets on a bike, totally focused on victory, is something else that brings me out in a cold sweat, notwithstanding the lighter traffic. And at least once I shocked them all by actually winning. Perhaps, with the ball and the need to run removed, I wasn't quite the tragic case I otherwise looked.

It also emerged that another sport I was less bad at was swimming. Although never placed, I did get picked for one or two galas and it was at the

Lifeboys' event on November 22nd 1963 that I had my JFK Moment. That's where I was when I heard, from my mother, that the American President had been shot. Aged 10, I didn't quite see what the panic was about, but aged 10 I also didn't appreciate the leadership the United States gave to the Western World such as JFK's role in the Cuba Missile Crisis just a year earlier.

My parents were very keen that I should learn to swim and I was soon taken to "The Baths" for lessons from Donnie Ross, one of several well known and generally popular attendants. They were easily picked out by their dark blue trousers and white T-shirts with a blue ring round the neck. "The Public Baths" had become a bit of an anachronism by the 60s, when most houses had their own, but you could still go there for a bath in the area opposite the cash desk. However most went straight up to the swimming pool.

We would dash out of school at 3:55 and jump on the 4 o'clock bus which took us from the school gate to Academy Street. At the pool in Friars Place we would present one of Inverness Town Council's finest creations, the Baths Card. These were distributed through schools and entitled holders to free admission, each registered by a tick in the 10x10 grid of small squares. A swim would normally have cost around 6d, so it was a great saver and a fine promoter of swimming for fitness and as a sport. Opened during the 1930s to replace premises on Montague Row, this 100 foot pool ran from a three foot shallow end up to nine feet at the deep end. Managed by Bill Morrison, it was still relatively state of the art. Disinfected by "breakpoint chlorination", whose afterglow would linger on in your nostrils for hours.

It had a one metre and a three metre board and diving head first from "the top board" was something of a juvenile rite of passage.

Changing was in cubicles up the length of the pool - males to the right and females to the left. You collected a numbered wire basket from a kiosk and then returned it, filled with your clothes and shoes. Washing feet in sinks at the shallow end was required but often not enforced and on your way out, or if you felt cold in the middle of your swim, there were wonderful hot showers. The pool was also heated so the energy use of the place must have been phenomenal.

General sessions weren't really for serious swimmers who would attend clubs such as the LMS of an evening and there was also a ladies' night. Galas and water polo also took up time, and Inverness had a champion diver called Maurice Campbell. Late afternoons saw the pool in general mayhem, mainly with kids larking about with their worst excesses curbed by Ronnie Ross, Rod Dyce or one of the others.

These attendants also kept an eye on how long you had been in the water because during holidays we would go for the whole afternoon if we could. They would demand to see the palms of your hands and wrinkled fingertips meant you'd been in too long and you got your marching orders. Once dressed, there was sometimes a visit to the shop in the upper gallery for a puff candy or some other tooth destroyer. More often it was chips from the Academy Street chipper (best in town, I thought) if you were getting the bus home, or Serafini's in Tomnahurich Street (choice of a 4d or a 6d bag) if you were walking.

The big highlight of the week was the Saturday afternoon pilgrimage to Telford Street Park to support Caledonian FC, which many from Dalneigh did. Our own game behind Kavvies' was followed by a quick lunch before heading off before 1:30 for a 3pm kick off. Our route to the ground was up Lilac Grove, through a lane to Fairfield Road and down Balnacraig Road (known to older Inveressians as Bumber's Lane) which was still an unmetalled dustbowl if it wasn't a quagmire.

You would have thought that such enthusiastic Caley fans - members indeed of the recently revived Supporters' Club - would have been more than keen to pay their Juvenile admission of 9d at the turnstile, but not a bit of it. The normal means of entry was "Joopeen in over the gate" on the back corner of the ground beside Howden's nurseries. We were never caught, but nor were there too many people around over an hour before kickoff.

Free entry achieved, we would then increase our financial gain by combing the ground for small MacKintosh's lemonade bottles left lying around after the previous game. These may have been unimportant to their original purchasers but they could be cashed in for 3d apiece at the shop by the main gate. This would normally net enough for some McCowans Penny Dainties or Cow Toffee and a bag of Smiths' crisps with the little blue twist of salt. Any surplus would go towards entry to the front stalls at the Playhouse or La Scala the following Saturday when Caley were away.

Our early arrival also meant having to endure the truly awful Scottish Country Dance music that assailed the ground through tinny tannoys, but the teams soon came out to great applause, not least from us. This was a successful period for Caley and our last three years in primary school each produced a top three league finish. Brora Rangers had just joined to make a 16 team Highland League which Caley won in 1964. The side scored an average of three goals a game so there was no shortage of celebration. That celebration could sometimes challenge young teeth if it became necessary to cheer for a goal with them embedded in a Penny Dainty, which was actually enormous enough to cause "hamster cheeks" when wedged in sideways.

At half time we would usually move from the Howden End to the Distillery (later the Comet) End or vice versa to be right on the spot if, or usually when, Caley scored. It was amid the passion of a packed Howden End that I first experienced the combined aroma of whisky and cigarette smoke whilst gaining exotic extensions to my vocabulary. As full time approached, autograph books would come out of pockets during a further journey to the front of the stand. There we would luxuriate in the smell of hot pies wafting out of the tunnel as we waited for a signature from Davie Reid or Jimmy Smith or Ian Nelson. Over 30 years later, in October 1996, I attended the last football match ever to be played at Telford Street Park. There I wallowed in a wave of nostalgia, not the least from that pie smell which had changed not one bit.

Autographs obtained, it was back up Balnacraig Road for tea and Dr Who which competed with the Highland League results on Grampian TV. Then there might be a walk to Lawson's shop for the Football Times which provided an extensive run down of the day's games.

It was as a "copy boy" for the Football Times that another of our schoolmates, David Love, cut his teeth on his family profession of journalism which would become his own for life. For decades, in order to get copy from the earlier stages of games at the three Inverness grounds to the FT office in Diriebught Road, the paper employed boys on bikes to collect sheets of paper from match reporters and pedal like fury across town before returning for the next instalment. Given the lack of communications technology, the Football Times did a remarkable job hitting the streets as soon as it did, around two hours after final whistles, or possibly even less.

Occasionally, and usually only if Caley were playing their town rivals away, we would visit Clach Park or Thistle's ground at Kingsmills. Before they had to sell bits of it off to cover crippling debt, Clach's Grant Street Park was vast, with three stands or enclosures and the Wine Shed. I never personally saw the legendary "Mackles" racing his whippet up and down the pitch at half time, but this epitomised community spirit "down the Merkinch", and Clach FC was at the heart of that.

Kingsmills was rather less impressive and witnessed less success before manager King Willie Grant led the Jags to back to back Highland League titles in 1972 and 1973. The ground still hadn't begun the desperate physical decline which had set in by the early 1990s. This would see Kingsmills initially adopted as Caley Thistle's temporary first home before that idea had to be abandoned in view of the sheer awfulness of the place. It did, however, have a very good pie shop in a black and red hut which ended its life, post Thistle, as a garage near the Bught Park. Visits to both these grounds provided frequent satisfaction for title chasing Caley fans in the mid-60s when Clach hovered mid table while Thistle languished at or near the bottom before the club's revival under chairman Jock McDonald.

Many other Saturday afternoons were spent at the "pictures". The term derives from the original title "moving pictures" which the Americans shortened to "movies" and indeed "cinema" is a relatively new term. For a shilling you could get into the front stalls at the La Scala which was still referred to as a "picture house". The Playhouse was rather more expensive and the Front Balcony, where my dad used to take me to see blockbusters like The Great Escape, Lawrence of Arabia, Dr Zhivago or The Longest Day, was 6 shillings or even seven and six. Otherwise, the proceeds of our Telford Street bottle collections would allow us, with a bit of neck craning, to see current favourites like Mary Poppins or Goldfinger or Help! or a good old fashioned cowboy film. The La Scala was considered the lesser of the two Inverness picture houses and the urban myth was that it was riddled with fleas. I never experienced any but certainly saw a lot of good films there.

What we did get were lungsful of cigarette smoke which also picked out the projector beam like a searchlight. You always knew when the "B" film was approaching an end because a girl (or at least usually a girl) in uniform would walk down the aisle carrying round her neck a tray lit by a small lamp and full of ice cream. The La Scala also hosted a Saturday morning matinée but I never particularly wanted to go. The lure of the Back O' Kavvies was probably too strong.

One summer we even went fruit picking at Lentran to earn a little money, making this my first paid employment. Many of the strawberries ended up in our stomachs and this sweated labour didn't yield much cash so was rejected after a very few days. When we did go, it was unsupervised on the bus, although once we all walked back into Inverness on what was still the main A9.

Then there was the occasional summer day trip to Craig Phadrig. We would cross the canal - where another rite of passage was the ability to throw a stone right across - and head up through the open country where the Kinmylies housing estate was later built. Lunch would be taken at King Brude's vitrified fort at the summit before a descent on the Clachnaharry side of the hill.

One day, just at the Clachnaharry railway bridge, we met a group who were shouting "We are the Ferry Gang", which certainly terrified me, partly because if it came to flight, I wasn't best placed. When I got home, I told my parents who managed to persuade me that there was a fairy glen around there and they were shouting "We are the FAIRY gang."

Somehow, I don't think so, and there was some apprehension among Dalneigh youth about getting on the wrong side of South Kessock's more aggressive characters. I only ever experienced this once, some years later, but we made our escape to safety. Especially feared in the mid-60s was a boy called Billy Hargreaves - who went on to become a highly respected police officer and is an absolute gentleman. Yes, of course The Ferry had more than its fair share of problem - and indeed also deprived - families but in the main it was, and still is, well populated by some of the nicest, most genuine and friendly people you could meet.

Some of our other activities were rather less innocent than lunching on Craig Phadrig. There was nothing fundamentally evil but, as a group, we were sometimes a complete nuisance in the community. Strangely, apart from one incident, we were never caught so our parents were totally unaware of our less savoury goings on.

Penny Bangers went on sale long before Guy Fawkes night and we usually bought them singly or in boxes of a dozen for a shilling. These were pretty powerful, comprising the legendary "blue touch paper", then a section that fizzed to allow you to "stand well clear" and finally a cylindrical chamber with the powder that gave quite a prodigious bang. Adults and pets must have dreaded Guy Fawkes night since for weeks before it, bangers would be "let off" all over the place.

The "genies" occasionally made with bigger and more expensive fireworks were far more popular with the penny banger where you split the case, poured the powder out on the kerb and threw a lit match on to it to create a great flash and a huge puff of smoke.

It was more usual to use bangers in their more conventional form - sometimes by lighting them, waiting for the fizz to start and throwing them up a path on to someone's front doorstep before legging it away at maximum speed. As the slowest runner, I was seldom called upon to throw the banger and was usually allowed to make my escape a second or two before the rest. By this time of year, it got dark quite early, which increased our chances of getting away with it. In reality, it was just all too easy for a group of offenders to evaporate into the rabbit warren of narrow paths which linked the streets and garage blocks of Dalneigh.

How this casual use of explosives never resulted in injury, I just don't know and that was before you even thought about the tuppeny banger, a real thunderflash which, perhaps mercifully, wasn't so readily available. Someone even blitzed a wasps' nest in the wall at the garages by inserting one through its narrow entrance. And then there was the time that one brave individual placed a Roman Candle in our Primary 5 teacher Mrs Anderson's front hedge, set it going and did a runner.

I have to admit that errant pyrotechnics were just one of our transgressions. The Reverend Hamish MacIntyre had a huge garden around his manse with several trees, including one which produced a lot of apples. This provided the means for another of our seasonal activities known as "Nicking The Minister's (or 'The Minnie's') Apples". However this particular activity was widespread.

For kids on the other side of Dalneigh, the equivalent sport was "Nicking the Sheriff's Apples". A local Sheriff, Stanley Scott Robinson I believe, lived on Dochfour Drive at the corner of Caledonian Road and despite his legal status, his apples were as vulnerable as the Reverend MacIntyre's.

The manse apple tree grew right beside one of the blocks of lock ups, so it was easy to climb up and reach it from there. Indeed in the middle of one apple raid, a girl even fell off the garage roof into a neighboring garden causing all manner of panic. Some of our ill-gotten gains were eaten, occasionally at the expense of a sore stomach next day because most of the apples were green. Meanwhile others, those verging upon rotten, were stored up and used as ammunition to throw at the front doors of unsuspecting residents.

These were often the same poor souls whose premises would be assailed again by bangers in the weeks to come, but we still had no moral qualms about a further visit at Hallowe'en seeking hospitality. Indeed it's more than possible that the ammunition for the final days of the banger campaign was purchased with the victims' very Hallowe'en generosity.

There was never any vandalism or evil intent and any house with an elderly person was scrupulously spared. But although I don't remember any breakages, throwing apples at doors with glass panels was pretty risky. Despite that lack of malice, we were still a public nuisance and I have never understood why there was no police presence around Dalneigh during dark, early evening hours.

Then there were the steel doors of the St Ninian Drive garages. We would often play on the garage roofs and annoy the chap who lived in the house nearest them. His kids were often trying to get to sleep and we weren't helping at all.

I suppose you could argue about the dividing line between our intransigence and his intolerance when he would suddenly appear and tell us "Here! Cut out the noise!", earning him the nickname "Less Noise". But the real problem arose when, as his disapproval escalated, so did our behaviour. Eventually we started climbing up on the garage roofs with our feet hanging over the edge, hammering our heels thunderously on the steel doors and running away before he could get out into his garden.

After a week or two, "Less Noise" lost patience and went and complained to my parents. They took the view that yes, we were out of order but "Less Noise" could have dealt with the initial situation more diplomatically and not provoked escalation. Five or six years later, as an under age drinker, I would see "Less Noise" again as a member of a very popular band in one of the town's up market drinking establishments.

I declined one activity completely, mainly due to my complete lack of athleticism. There was a large hedge between our garden and other half of our semi, by then occupied by Bill Jack the Burgh Architect, but the other gardens were only separated by wire fences about two and a half feet high. This led to Beys, Brems, Kavvies and one or two others holding races in the pitch dark, starting on my back lawn and ending up in one on St Mungo Road, some seven gardens away. It was again amazing that no one was caught and the only trouble our band of delinquents ever got into was with "Less Noise"

With hindsight, do I have regrets about behaving like this? Well... yes I do. It's very easy to judge the practices of a previous age by later standards, but I think this was unacceptable by any measure and I was probably letting my unsuspecting parents down here. But this was just what young boys did and we had no previous experience of any other norm.

One quite sad aspect of this memorable group friendship was how quickly we drifted apart after going to separate secondary schools and separate classes. I bumped into Brems for the first time in decades in the Caley Club one night; Beys' niece and my daughter became very good friends so, on one of his trips home from South Africa, she arranged for us to meet up; I used to spot Kavvies at these acrimonious football merger meetings in the early 1990s. But I have seen, usually at the gym, a bit more of Roddy who provided the photograph in this book of our Primary 7 class.

As an introduction to the idea of camaraderie among a group of friends, I could have hoped for no better than these Dalneigh boys.

CHAPTER 5 – DALNEIGH SCHOOL.

Many people retain a clear memory of their first day at school and I am no different. My mother walked me, in my new black blazer with red braid and school cap, up from Kenneth Street and, with the other mums, came with me into Dalneigh's large assembly hall with its well equipped stage. We entered by the Primary 1 and 2 door at the church end of the building, walked along the corridor and into that hall to be introduced to my first teacher, Miss Ena MacKenzie, bedecked in a flowery dress which was the height of late 1950s fashion.

At this point, the mothers left; some children cried, but I didn't and we were placed in our classes. For the first two years these were allocated by age so I was in the July to December group in Room 3. Next door in Room 4 was the January to June class with Miss Kathleen MacKintosh whom I knew as a friend of my aunt and uncle. Among the other infant staff was Miss Nan Young, sister of Charlie Young, a well known figure in the Baptist Church who also worked alongside my father.

Within these first few minutes I had seen as much of Dalneigh Primary School as I would during the next two years in the infant department. Beyond that corridor and the hall stretched a symmetrical wing with Rooms 5 to 8 and behind the hall, much of it upstairs, there was a large L-shaped block with Rooms 9-16 and a General Purposes Room. Even the oldest part of the building had only been there for four years so the place was pretty well pristine. And surrounding it all was a wire mesh fence, about four feet high, which kept half the scheme awake at night when the wind whistled through it.

Dalneigh Primary School

The corridor floors, which had an ever repeating pattern, were kept extremely shiny by Mr MacKenzie the janitor and there was a very fresh smell throughout. Indeed the floors were so shiny that kids in their stocking soles could and did take a run up and slide for several yards along them. The idea was that everyone wore black sandshoes which you took out of a compartment beneath your coat peg in the morning and exchanged for your outdoor shoes. However, some didn't wear sandshoes - perhaps because families couldn't afford them, but perhaps not.

Mr MacKenzie also kept the toilets spotless, rounding off the job with some kind of industrial strength disinfectant, judging by the smell. The

School tie and badge

only down side of the toilets was the decidedly non-absorbent Izal toilet paper, which smelt of disinfectant and could be very abrasive to a pre-pubescent sphincter. One of the great philosophical questions of early school years was why the girls' toilets reputedly had far more cubicles but no urinals.

The most conspicuous feature of Room 3 and indeed all the classrooms was the huge multi-paned windows. These were part of the school's modern, 1950s design and they certainly let in a lot of daylight. This was in complete contrast with older, Victorian schools where the impression was of being taught in a dungeon, with much smaller windows located well above head height. The other notable thing about Room 3 was a large cardboard panel divided into 26 squares, one for each letter of the alphabet, written in both lower and upper cases.

The strange thing about going through Dalneigh School was that time seemed constantly to decelerate. The first two years are a fairly fleeting memory while the last two, in common with these extra mural activitles such as bonfires and nicking the Minister's apples, are remembered as a blissful eternity.

Primaries 1 and 2 were both with Miss MacKenzie, who later became Mrs MacAskill and had a son who was among my first pupils at Inverness Royal Academy. These two years passed in a very pleasant blur of red and blue counters, rudimentary reading, writing and number and sitting cross legged on the floor at the teacher's desk to be read a story.

There was also a constant awareness of Miss MacLean who had an office just along the corridor and whose wrath we all felt when we were left outside in our lines a little longer than usual and we took up the chant "We want in!". As you proceeded into the building, you were expected to salute the teacher on door duty. I remember my dad, ex-Seaforth Highlander as he was, remarking that this really shouldn't be happening - not because he objected to the principle, but only Americans saluted when not wearing head gear! If there was a teacher on each side, many of us used to salute with both hands at once!

Primary 3 inevitably resulted in more advanced work in classes split for the first time into A and B sets. The 3A teacher in Room 7 was the charismatic Miss Margaret Cameron whom we all loved. Educationally she was quite progressive and went on to work at Moray House College of Education, a move which cost us a second year with her. Our motivation was sky high; Margaret Cameron just had that something that inspired you to learn.

It was in P3 that we first encountered joined up writing and that in itself was groundbreaking. Gone were the traditional loops and whirls which were replaced by a more modern script known as Marion Richardson Writing.

Pupil group - Dalneigh Primary School - around 1964

This was still joined up, but the likes of the "f", "l" and "b" had open ends so the pencil sometimes needed to come away from the paper. It was an altogether simpler style so probably a life saver for me since, even using this, my handwriting is still all but illegible.

It was also in P3 that we were first introduced to

the already moribund pen and inkpot. Ball point pens, also called Biros, were now fairly commonplace alongside fountain pens with their own ink cartridges. Scratchy metal nibs, the next step up after a goose feather quill and dipped into an ink well, really were obsolete, but practice with them would continue right through primary school.

Pen and inkwell are a nightmare for left handers. The world is designed for the 85% of the population who are right handed. We therefore write from left to right so a right hand holding a pen leads rather than follows the script. A left hander has the opposite experience, constantly smearing the still wet ink over what has just been written. Similarly, desks always had inkwell holes in the far right corner. A left handed person therefore had to stretch diagonally to replenish their nib after every few words, hugely increasing the likelihood that the dark blue liquid, concocted from ink powder and water, would dribble over the page on the way back. But at least the days of tying left hands behind backs to force children to write with their right hand were long gone.

Times tables, rejected by a later generation of educators and then reinstated in view of the resulting damage, were memorised at a steady rate alongside ever more challenging addition, subtraction and multiplication. Division - even the short variety - was more complex and demanding, and always lagged that bit further behind.

The great fascination and indeed revelation of P3 was the class library. It was nothing elaborate from the outside - simply something that might today have been taken for a hinged Ikea flat pack, but it opened out to reveal a treasure trove of children's literature which belied its compactness. The packed

shelves of Miss Cameron's library also gave me my first encounter with Ladybird books, and in particular their range of historical biographies.
Admiral Nelson, Queen Elizabeth I, Alfred The Great, Florence Nightingale and many more. Yes, they were predominantly English but that was probably an issue of availability rather than educational policy since at Dalneigh, Scottish history was taught throughout.

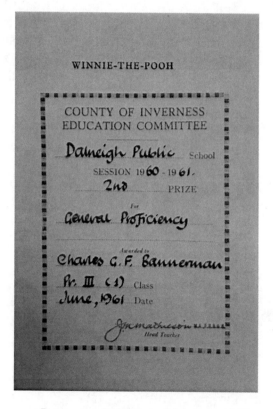

Runner up in Primary 3A - June 1961

Dalneigh Primary staff mid-1960s with Head Teacher John MacLeod front centre.

One particular favourite was a rather larger volume about the Vikings. I would give this P3 class library, soon to be reinforced by the Children's Britannica at home, much of the credit for inspiring a life long interest in history.

Achievements were rewarded by gold and silver stars on a big board at the back of the room and at the end of a year of great educational progress, I received my first school prize. My reward for finishing second in the class to Iain Steven - a 1-2 that would be repeated in all the other twice yearly class exams throughout Dalneigh School - was a hardback copy of AA Milne's Winnie The Poo.

It was at this point, in 1961, that Dalneigh's Head Teacher John Mathieson left to become first head of the new Millburn Junior Secondary, which eventually evolved into the comprehensive known as Millburn

Academy. He was replaced by John MacLeod, a
Drumnadrochit man who later went on to become
Assistant Director of Education at Highland Regional
Council. At such an early stage I had barely known
John Mathieson but got to know his successor a good
deal better as the years went by and I developed a
great admiration for him.

When I applied for my first teaching job in 1976,
my interview was conducted by Divisional Education
Officer Ivor Sutherland and I was able to read upside
down on his papers that John MacLeod had
recommended me for a post.

We were all disappointed when Miss Cameron,
who would otherwise have taken us in P4 as well, left
at the end of session 1960-61. However, she had an
admirable replacement in Miss Rena Fraser who,
after many years at Dalneigh, progressed to become
Assistant Head Teacher at Lochardil. The other
occupants of that P3/4 wing included Mrs Hill, Miss
Charles, Miss MacFadyen and the diminutive and
occasionally fierce Mrs Notman.

Once again the level of work progressed across
all fronts and Miss Fraser was very keen on Mental
Arithmetic. Apart from regular exercises and class
tests she also held competitions. Here two pupils
would go head-to-head in a "first to answer - best of
three" contest. Questions might typically have been
"What's the cost of eight bars of chocolate at
fourpence each?" or "How many inches in two feet
five inches". The loser would sit down while someone
else would then come out to face the winner. On one
occasion I went round the entire class unbeaten and
began to realise that mental arithmetic was
emerging as one of my strong points.

As in previous years, PE - which was still called

"gym" - had a regular place in the curriculum. There was a specialist visiting teacher, Mrs Turnbull, who put us through various primitive, synchronised evolutions which fully explained why PE teachers used to be called "drillies". But this had at least evolved from the even more conventional "drill" of previous generations, such as my father remembered at Bell's School in the 1920s from local strongman and entertainer Donald Dallas... wearing "tackety boots".

Boys wore short trousers right through primary school and these sufficed for gym classes, but the girls were required to attend in "navy blue knickers". A garment more unbecoming than these thick, baggy creations is difficult to imagine. They must have been as embarrassing to their wearers as National Health specs with their round lenses and springy clips which dug holes into the back of the ears. Sometimes Mrs Turnbull would wear similar knickers to the girls', but with two differences. Hers were green, so possibly a relic of her training at Dunfermline College, and she filled them considerably more amply!

The wearing of short trousers right through primary school, and indeed I was one of the minority who also wore them for a brief period in secondary, was par for the course in an era when kids' clothes hadn't quite acquired the elegance afforded by synthetic fibres. Woolly hand knitted jumpers and cardigans – often hand-me-downs – were the order of the day and wool is quite easily pulled out of shape. Older garments, especially when the elbows had been mended, therefore looked quite scruffy and could therefore create an impression of poverty. Not infrequently, at a time when the life of school blazers was also extended by leather elbow patches, that was actually the reason and class photos often give the impression of quite a motley crew. The era of throwaway extravagance was still some way off.

For Primary 5, we had to move the length of the school to Room 10 and another superb teacher, Mrs Anderson. By now a series of memories has begun to coalesce into a more coherent thread. Religious Education had a preserved place in the curriculum and this was one of many things Mrs Anderson did very well. She was greatly assisted by a series of exquisitely worked posters which went through the Old Testament chronologically - Abraham, Moses, David, Elijah and so on - and these accompanied the narrative of the lessons.

Arithmetic had by then progressed to the ultimate challenge of long division which now hasn't generally been taught in schools for years, but it provided very demanding cerebral training sessions. Interpretations and "compositions" also loomed large because we were now well into the latter half of what 1960s primary education was principally about - the Promotion Exam, sometimes called The 11 Plus. This was sat towards the end of P7 and would decide the nature of each and every child's secondary education. In the Spring of 1963, for reasons best known to herself, Mrs Anderson unofficially gave both Iain and me that year's papers just to see how we would do. After she marked them, she told us we had actually passed two years early.

It wasn't all sweetness and light with Mrs Anderson, though, because she was also the first teacher (among only three) to give me the belt. It wasn't that the belt was absent further down the school; we were just lucky only to be encountering it now. Use of the belt was incredibly varied and arbitrary. For instance in Crown school there was a woman who was said, possibly Apocryphally, to have taught with the Bible in one hand and the belt in the other!

Almost four decades after the practice was abolished, it's sometimes very difficult to get the younger generation to believe that the law used to allow teachers to thrash the palms of pupils' hands in doses of up to six strokes using a hefty strip of leather manufactured specially by a Mr Dick of Lochgelly in Fife.

I now have to pinch myself in order to believe that this was normal then, if not always commonplace. Even by the 60s corporal punishment wasn't being used as liberally or as viciously as before and in the 1950s, Royal Academy Rector D J MacDonald issued an edict that "girls are not to be strapped". (If the belt was still in use today, this could presumably be challenged on the grounds of sex discrimination.)

But it had by no means died out and would not do so until the early 80s. Some teachers - and it was said that Inverness High School "Teckies" were prominent among them - were still notorious for the efficiency and frequency with which they wielded leather. This was less the case with Mrs Anderson and on the few occasions I got it from her, it didn't really hurt. Or maybe, dealing with nine and ten year olds, she just held back.

The following year proved to be something of a different ball game because the belt from Mrs Ballantyne was a rather more rigorous experience, even though she used a "two tonguer" as opposed to Mrs Anderson's "three tonguer". That actually did hurt quite a lot, with the dull ache on red palms persisting for maybe an hour or more after the shock of the initial impact. It was also said to be much more painful if administered on cold hands after snowballing offences. Different teachers had different techniques. Straight on carried the risk of damaging wrists and presented a narrower target, so many gave it sideways. Then there were "double handers" where you had to put out one hand below the other in order to increase resistance to the downward stroke.

I never, on the other hand, witnessed anywhere what was surely the most unjust use of corporal punishment – for poor academic performance. There were some teachers who would use the belt on any poor kid who got more than two or three spellings wrong or whatever. Punishing lack of academic ability like that was unforgivable and must have led to some poor children spending much of their school time in fear of pain on account of something over which they had absolutely no control.

I didn't get the belt very often from Mrs Ballantyne but there was no question of my getting an easy passage because she had been a neighbour and was my mother's friend. The same applied to the time I was called out to give details for my end of year prize and was caught taking a sneak peek at the 7/6d price label on the book. That resulted in a hefty slap right on the top of the head.

Primary 5 was punctuated by a famously freezing, snowbound winter. There was enduring, deep snow, often well past my waist, from January 1963 right through to March. Negotiating the quarter mile to school was a major challenge, made that bit easier when some kind soul cleared the St Ninian Drive grass up to the school gate. It was still intimidating walking through that corridor, with excavated snow piled up above head height.

When the snow was less deep, it was ideal for making "slides". If you slid along a stretch of it often enough, the pressure would compact it into an icy film which it was great fun to slide down. Often the playground would have several parallel slides each several yards long made by various groups – until Mr MacKenzie applied sand and salt and ruined them.

There were visiting teachers for subjects other than PE. Our Art teacher in P5 was Margaret Cameron's sister Jackie who was just as much of a gem. When unavailable, Jackie Cameron was replaced by a ghastly woman known as "Kipperfeet". She was so hopeless that after she had departed, usually in a temper because we couldn't understand what she was going on about, Mrs Anderson had to go over the whole thing with us again from scratch.

Art was very much in the list of practical activities that I was hopeless at, but on one famous occasion I did manage to beat the system. When we were in P7, Brooke Bond Tea held a modern art competition, with a prize awarded in each school. I had a vague idea of what "modern" art was, so I just did my usual - a horrible, non-descript melange of browns and greens and purples which was meant to represent a country road. But then there was my stroke of genius. On the road I daubed what looked vaguely like a van, but I made sure that the words "Brooke Bond Tea" were clearly legible on it and this seemed to do the trick. A few weeks later, it emerged that I had won the prize - to the hysterical amusement of everybody else in the class! This only reinforced my belief that "modern art" can quite easily be created by a handless kid randomly splashing paint around and pulling the "experts'" legs.

The visiting music teacher was an Englishman called John Mallinson who was well known in local musical circles. He was quite elderly, small in stature and bald on top with a grey surround and had a strange manner which was simultaneously funny and a bit threatening. He therefore got a mixed reception from pupils but, because I was interested in music, I gave him the benefit of the doubt. Music classes were held in the large General Purposes Room.

If someone slightly misbehaved, he would grab their leg just above the kneecap and squeeze, which activated a "tickle reflex". More serious offenders, including on one famous occasion Davie Love, saw the miscreant put in the walk-in store cupboard. However, when Malllinson left the room, Davie put on the teacher's coat and trilby hat, came out of the cupboard and began to impersonate him. Unfortunately, Davie's timing wasn't quite right and Mallinson returned sooner than expected, catching Davie in the act.

Six of the belt from John MacLeod was Davie's penance and this possibly acted as a partial deterrent to Dallas Fraser when he was similarly consigned. Only partial, though, because Dallas took a rubber from his pocket and tore it into small fragments which he placed in the trilby. Clearly it didn't occur to Dallas that the instant Mallinson put the hat on it would be quite obvious who the offender was, leading to further ructions.

One of John Mallinson's regular activities involved a sol-fa modulator. This white canvas strip with black writing hung from the side of the blackboard and it had the sol-fa scale on it - that's "doh a deer" and so on, as in The Sound Of Music. He would point to various notes, usually of a Psalm tune, and the class would have to sing the tune as he went along. For instance the" Old 100th" was "Doh, doh, te, la, soh, do, ray, me. Me, me, me, ray, do, fah, me, ray......"

Sometimes he would get pupils to come out to do this with the class singing along to what was being pointed out on the modulator, and when it was my turn, he went into sudden raptures about my performance. What I didn't admit was that for years I had been standing beside my dad in church as he sang from his own sol-fa hymn book, so I was very familiar with the tunes and with sol-fa.

On the GP room wall were various posters of great composers like Mendelssohn, Beethoven and Vaughan Williams and my fascination with these was an early indication of my keenness on classical music. When we then went to a Scottish National Orchestra concert in the High School, where we had to sing Parry's "Jerusalem", I found myself enthralled. At this time a few songs in the charts borrowed classical tunes and this also intrigued me. So did Paul McCartney's string quartet compositions within Beatles songs like "Eleanor Rigby".

Mallinson also trained school choirs for the Inverness Music Festival, but I once fell foul of him for not paying attention and was excluded, but took a gamble that I would be reinstated, so didn't tell my parents. There was a bit of brinkmanship here since I was only allowed back in on the morning of the competition with my mother already on her way to the Town House to watch me.

Because my mother didn't work, I always went home for lunch so had no great experience of "school dinners". Once or twice I had to go if my parents were at a wedding or a funeral but that was about it. Unless a child qualified for free meals, tickets were a shilling for the first member of the family. It was 11d for the next, followed by 10d and 9d for very large broods, with tickets dispensed from rolls of different colours.

Primaries 6 and 7, in Room 10, seem to merge into a single, highly fulfilling and enjoyable episode and this continuity was helped on its way by having the same teacher. The single aim of both school sessions - the Promotion Exam in February 1965 - also reinforced the feeling.

Mrs Ballantyne certainly upped the level of work again; some of it really was quite demanding for children of our age, but many of us thrived on it. English interpretations stretched us right out, especially ones where coloured cards were retrieved from a box and when you had mastered one colour you moved on to the next. "Meanings" and "Spelling" also had to be memorised for homework after being copied from the board, and compositions were written. We had a textbook called "Essentials of English", packed with everything from comparatives and superlatives to collective nouns such as an "exultation" of larks and a "murder" of crows. Like other books and jotters, it was dutifully covered with brown paper or spare wallpaper.

What might really shock modern day pupils - and indeed their teachers as well - was the level at which grammar was taught. Nouns, verbs, adjectives and adverbs - of manner, place, time and degree - oh yes, and conjunctions, were just the start. Then there were subjects and predicates the Particular Analysis of words and the General Analysis of

Sentences. This really was heavy duty stuff, often given for homework, where tables had to be drawn and principal clauses distinguished from a variety of subordinate ones. Grammar also afforded several opportunities to learn through the whole class repeatedly chanting definitions like "A verb is a doing word". The teacher would then say "Again!" and so the cycles continued.

However this just turned out to be the start of a grammatical journey. Primary school grammar then made French and Latin a lot easier in secondary school and that in turn led to an even better grasp of English grammar and all its implications for speech and writing.

Mid-1960s Primary 6 and 7 arithmetic would also frighten the modern generation. Not only did it require a high level of numeracy without the aid of a calculator, it was further complicated by the almost complete absence of convenient multipliers and divisors of 10. Imperial units were still alive and well so we had to learn a whole range of different tables, which were found on the back of our brown Buck's Head jotters.

Sixteen ounces one pound... 14 pounds one stone... 8 stones one hundredweight... 20 hundredweights one ton. Twelve inches one foot.... 3 feet one yard.... 220 yards one furlong (or 22 to the chain)... 8 furlongs one mile. Twelve pennies one shilling... 20 shillings one pound, and there were various other values like the half crown and the florin. With the crown and the farthing now gone, one of each of the remaining seven coins still in use added up to 6s 41/2d. Occasionally questions would involve the guinea, valued at £1 1s and sometimes used in charging for professional services. Then there was the "gross" numbering 144, or 12 dozen articles.

Imperial units made "Bills" a frequent challenge but housewives and shop assistants alike had to be able to work this kind of thing out for themselves. We were regularly confronted with bills for stuff like "Three and a half yards of ribbon at 4d per foot; 2 stone 6lb of potatoes at tuppence ha'penny a pound; 6 ounces of tea at 3/4d per pound; Half a gross of clothes pegs at 5d for three. (Try it – the answer should be £1 1s 10d.)

Class 7A, Dalneigh Primary School 1964 - 65

On Friday mornings in Primary 7, we were given a past Promotion Arithmetic paper to do and this would also include long division - stuff like 3656 divided by 23 with the odds usually just expressed as a remainder. Long multiplication such as 638 x 36 had to be set out in the proper manner and there were also quite demanding problems. For instance you could be given the dimensions of the front of a house and of its door and two windows and be asked to work out the wall area. This could be quite a challenge when working in feet and inches! Then there was "If six men (always men) dig a hole in four days, how long would it take eight men to dig the same hole?", which is inverse proportion in disguise.

Latterly in P7, Mrs Ballantyne started giving Iain and me some maths above and beyond the Promotion syllabus. This included using "pi" to work out circumfrences and areas of circles and we once found an answer at the back of the book which was wrong. When we queried this with her, she suggested that we go and see Mr MacLeod.

On our arrival at the Headmaster's office, he did indeed seem a bit nonplussed - to the extent that he just seemed vaguely to agree with us. Nora Ballantyne later told my mother that we had gone to the wrong Mr MacLeod; she had intended us to go to the Depute Head who was also called John MacLeod and taught 7B in Room 15. He was an real mathematician whereas his boss had a degree in Arts with no great inclination towards the kind of numeracy to which we were aspiring.

The 7B John MacLeod, a Gaelic speaker from Harris, took the Gaelic choir but wouldn't tell us what the phonetics we were singing actually meant, which seriously questioned the point of the whole exercise. He didn't have a house of his own but lived in the Moyness Hotel at the bottom of Bruce Gardens and walked to school from there.

There were also liberal helpings of History (much of it Scottish History including the sticky ends of the first four James Stewarts) and Geography, a minimal amount of Science and no modern languages. I am in little doubt that we moved on from Dalneigh School with an excellent grounding in the 3Rs as well as a good working knowledge of several other subjects.

There was a lot of rote learning, especially of the Bible and poetry. Scripture passages included all 13 verses of 1st Corinthians Chapter 13 ("Though I speak with the tongues....") and a horrendously Apocalyptic bit from Exodus Chapter 20 threatening Hell and Damnation on your great grandchildren if you "sinned". At least that's my current understanding of it. In primary school, when we had to chunter out these particular lines about "visiting the iniquities....", we all thought it was about paying a social call to some family down the street. In other words we just learned stuff by rote, often with little idea of what we were talking about.

I can still "arise and go now" to Innisfree, although I don't think I would be terribly handy with the "clay and wattles". We hadn't a clue what a "Quinquireme of Niniveh" was but were more familiar with the "Dirty British coaster" when it appeared on the horizon in the last verse of John Masefield's "Cargoes". And on many occasions over the years I have "wandered lonely as a cloud".... although we would sometimes corrupt that into wandering "lonely as MacLeod".

Then there was Handwork... at least for some. One morning a week, many of the boys were taken out to the large field in front of the school for football practice, aimed at assembling a strong school team. In addition to Beys and Brems, Dalneigh had other quite tidy players, including future Highland League stars such as John Allison, Alan Stevenson and Sandy Anderson.

I, however, was not one of them. My complete ineptitude at football relegated me to the Handwork group which was sent up to Miss Ogilvie in Room 12 for more creative activities. Unfortunately, I wasn't much good at handwork either and I concocted some ghastly edifices such as a large bottle with painted bits of paper stuck to it, horrifying my mother by taking it home in the guise of a table lamp. I later found out that Isobel Ogilvie apologised to my mum for even letting it out of the school. Around Halloween, the handwork class turned to carving out lanterns from a turnip. Pumpkins had not yet extended their alien influence across the Atlantic but I did make a decent job of the biggest turnip I was able to drag into school.

Fortunately, practical activities weren't included in the half yearly assessments. It was the established norm after each test to place the class (which numbered over 40) in rank order and then seat them top to bottom from back left to front right. However Iain never seemed to behave quite well enough to last more than a few days up at the back. He was frequently moved to the front row under the teacher's nose and replaced beside me by the previous occupant of his new seat. Perhaps Mrs Ballantyne saw a further benefit here because this placed two of the less academically gifted in seats where they could get some help from their neighbours.

Dalneigh School was well equipped with radio points where you just had to plug in a speaker and out came whichever station was selected in the Headmaster's office. This allowed us to go to the GP Room for Music and Movement where you had to create your own dance-like activities - not my scene either. Nor was Nature Study (biological sciences just didn't interest me) and when that was playing in class, I was one of a few who would unobtrusively do that night's homework under the desk, hence creating more football time.

The desks invariably had lids and you kept all your books, jotters etc in the compartment below. All you took away in your schoolbag (mine was a stout leather affair with two hefty buckles) was what you needed for homework that night. This left the desk containing a fair bit of your worldly goods.

Unfortunately the inside of my desk was a complete tip which I was totally incapable of sorting and this was often done for me by Audrey Grant. We had not been in the same class in P1 and 2 since Audrey has an early birthday but got to know each other later in Primary school. Of all my Dalneigh friends, I have probably seen more of Audrey over the years than anyone else since she was an extremely good sprinter (who beat nearly all the boys at Dalneigh). So although Audrey went to the High School, we became close Inverness Harriers clubmates, our daughters are now extremely good friends and our grandsons have even met up for an informal kick around.

Much more to my taste on school radio was Singing Together. Here you would be issued with a booklet of text and music so you could sing along with the radio programme. Most of it was folk song kind of stuff like Early One Morning, John Peel or Greensleeves, but over half a century later I wonder how on earth they got away with the lyrics of some of the songs. Although run of the mill then, a few would now cause uproar, especially among the Woke Community.

Some of the Singing Together content was, in hindsight, pretty risque. In this era of the Black and White Minstrels, we actually had to enunciate "De Camptown ladies sing dis song - doodah, doodah...." in the cod-African American vernacular, sometimes along with jazz hands - and that was by no means the worst. No one tuned a hair at Old Zip Coon and then you found 11 year old children in a Scottish classroom blasting out the N-word among the lyrics of Johnny Comes Down To Hilo. Meanwhile domestic abuse was extolled in the Wee Cooper Of Fife (nickettynacketty noo noo noo), including his wife-beating exploits when she refused to become a skiffy.

Nobody among the educators or at the BBC turned a hair at the use of material like this with young children because it was regarded as quite normal. For instance I was the owner of a book called Little Black Sambo which I was given because the author was called Helen Bannerman. Singing Together was pretty well universally loved by kids and one does have to smile at the irony of the ultra-PC BBC's past including such material.

By the mid-1950s, the world was beginning to get on top of poliomyelitis, a viral disease whose severe forms could cause paralysis or even death. A vaccine in the benevolent medium of a sugar cube had become widely available and I received mine, aged three or four, at the Central School. Two children in my class had had the disease. George Polworth was only incapacitated by that single lower leg caliper and could take part in many physical activities with just a slight limp. However, Ann Thomson had been much worse affected and wore two full leg braces which severely restricted her mobility. Both received special swimming lessons at the baths and every week the Rev Hamish MacIntyre would appear in our classroom to collect them in the dormobile which his own large family obliged him to run. The way in which they both made light of their disability was an example to all.

I spent more time making raffia mats with the Handwork group while the other kids went outside to practice for the Inter School Sports. My interest in athletics had been modestly kindled by live coverage of the 1964 Tokyo Olympics with its gold medals from Lynn Davies in the long jump and Ann Packer in the 800m. For the duration of these Games, the circular pathway that enclosed the electricity transformer outside my house became a track about 120 yards' length where Iain and I would re-enact the various distances, often several in a session. Now Iain wasn't the best of runners but was always ahead of me – as was the entire class at the school sports.

I was literally the slowest boy – possibly the slowest pupil – in the class and felt so out of things when I saw other kids with multiple red, yellow and blue ribbons on their chests for placing in various events. But I did know that it was far more efficient to do the sack race by taking small running steps than by jumping. I therefore got my mother to sew two sacks together to make a very wide one – and the ruse worked! In P7 I eventually won the sack race and was able to sport a coveted red ribbon.

At the Inter School Sports themselves Iain and I were adopted as chief cheer leaders for Team Dalneigh. Apart from making a great big banner we also, with apologies to the Seven Dwarves, composed a chant – "Dalneigh, Dalneigh, we'll take the shield away. We'll beat the Crown and bring them down. Dalneigh, Dalneigh!"

And so we did. In 1965, the Education Authority Shield for the Primary section was duly awarded to Dalneigh, ahead of Crown, and it was hung with honour outside the school hall. This was possibly the final achievement of a pretty talented year group. Many went on to academic distinction, others played football at higher levels and there were also some fine athletes. Audrey became one of the top junior sprinters of her era and Christine Reid was pretty quick as well, while Lorna Allan was a very good high jumper and some of the football boys could sprint a bit too.

This all followed great celebrations when we beat Crown in the Road Safety Quiz, and our team of four, of which I was one, earned the great privilege of a tour in a huge black Police car. Sheila MacIntyre and I were appointed the school's representatives on the local Road Safety Committee and were simply allowed to walk, unaccompanied and without any hint of a risk assessment, a mile to the Town House where the meetings took place in the Council Chamber. In P7, I was appointed Head Boy with Catherine Zajac as Head Girl and I proudly sported on my blazer lapel an enamel badge with my title on it. The role involved various ex-officio tasks, including presence at Assembly and the Headmaster once took me with him to operate the slide projector for a talk he was giving in the Cummings Hotel. Later he gave me half a crown, which rather overwhelmed me!

One P7 duty which involved all the boys (only the boys) in our class, was delivering the daily milk.

Dalneigh Inter School Sports team - May 1965

This was an era of free school milk for all primary and secondary pupils and the bottles, each one third of a pint and contained in metal crates, had to be distributed throughout the school by a rota of boys from their delivery point at the back door. This was a much valued perk since, apart from providing an escape from lessons, it also gave an opportunity to tour the school and wander into other classrooms.

The Promotion Exam, which we look at in the next chapter, was sat in February 1965. Secondary teachers then marked them early in March while their pupils got a couple of afternoons off and the results were announced in May. The final act was the Prize Giving where I was awarded the Kate MacLean medal for Proxime Accessit (runner up to the Dux).

These had been seven very happy years with extremely good teachers throughout, but the time had now come for a parting of the ways and a very different style of education.

CHAPTER 6 – THE GREAT CHAIN OF BEING.

The history of secondary education in Inverness is quite complex, involving a series of schools at a string of locations and various arrangements for filling them. Schools came and went from the 16th century onwards. By the 1960s, Bell's Institution in Farraline Park, Dr Raining's School at the top of the Raining Stairs - which later became "The Doc's" youth club - the Convent School at La Sagesse and the posh and private Heatherley had all gone. The Royal Academy's fee paying primary department finally wound down in 1961, which was also the year the new Millburn Junior Secondary opened at Diriebught.

In 1936 the High School, known mid-20th century as the Technical High School or the "Tecky", moved into the premises it still occupies in Montague Row. A complex reorganisation to comprehensive education occupied almost the entire 1970s and saw three secondary schools within a fully selective system become five local comprehensives.

Inverness Royal Academy originated in the monastic school set up around Friars Street in 1233, which gave way to a 16th century Grammar School. Founded in 1792 and catering for the entire 5-18 age range, the Royal Academy was overwhelmingly private until fees were abolished for S4-6 and then S1-3 after Education Acts in 1918 and 1944.

However, money was never the only route into the Academy. There were also various bursaries, such as the one my father was unable to take up due to the family's move to Wick. These provided a safety net which ensured that a clever child of limited means could still receive an academic education.

Inverness High School - also known as The Teckie.

After World War 2, with all secondary education now free, the Promotion Exam held sway. In Inverness this governed entry to three different course levels at two schools - three after Millburn opened.

The highest performers, perhaps the top 15-20% or so, gained the Academic course at the Royal Academy and the next slice went to the High School for Technical or Commercial courses. These were very largely gender specific, and the small number of boys doing Commercial did get a bit of a ribbing.

The respective courses there included what were known colloquially as "Tecky" and "Typeen" and it was also possible to do French, but not Latin.

Both the Commercial and Technical streams took in pupils from across the town as well as much of the surrounding area since education was a County and not a Town Council responsibility. Those who did least well in the Promotion exam received more basic General courses at a school determined by where they lived. On the west side of the River Ness, these were also at the High School, while it was to accommodate this stream on the east that Millburn Junior Secondary had been built.

Hierarchy dominated education - and, to some extent, society as well although that had been changing slowly since World War I. At Dalneigh, the Primary 1 and 2 classes were split by month of birth, which at age five is as good an indicator of development as any. From P3 onwards there was the A class and the B class and latterly a C class which was effectively a "remedial" group.

In our year, around 16 of us were selected for the Academy while most of the rest of 7A, sitting at desks in strict attainment order from top to 42nd, got Technical or Commercial courses. A small number received a general recommendation, along with most if not all in the lower classes. Even in Dalneigh, moves between A and B classes were quite rare; I only remember one shift from 7B to 7A and that created quite a lot of now unacceptable stigma and prejudice. The hierarchical principle continued into secondary where, once again, movement between schools was very infrequent if it happened at all.

Promotion English paper 1965 - quite challenging for 11 or 12 year olds

Academy pupils were further subdivided into A, B, C, and D classes and sometimes an E stream, with only the As and Bs deemed capable of Latin. There seems to have been slight year on year variation at the High School, possibly depending on numbers, but

135

typically the top sets were split into A1 to A4, with General pupils in B, C and D classes. The Academy stopped A to D streaming shortly before the transition to comprehensive education began in 1971.

The Great Chain Of Being is a philosophical creation of the Ancient Greeks and was later incorporated into Roman Catholic theology and society in general. The original Great Chain had God at the top, followed by various hierarchies of angels before it moved through humans, again ranked, and various other terrestrial creatures. It then proceeded into Hell and its sundry categories of Devils, with Satan at the bottom.

Feudal Systems are one instance of how this was then adopted by society. With the Church, and hence education, also buying into it, people "knew their place". The belief was that God had afforded you a particular status in life (an idea eagerly espoused by the clergy, monarchs and aristocrats) and you were pretty well stuck with that.

One of many fascinating insights into this is provided in the 1970s drama series Upstairs Downstairs by Hudson the butler who is an unshakeable believer that masters and servants were born to these unalterable roles. Hudson's natural successor, Carson in Downton Abbey, is of identical mould which makes it so difficult for him, for instance, to accept Milord's daughter marrying Branson the chauffeur.

The children's hymn "All Things Bright And Beautiful", written around 1850, contains the now astonishing verse: "The rich man in his castle, the poor man at his gate. God made them high and lowly, and ordered their estate." I have clear memories of singing this very verse myself, despite challenges from the 17th century onwards to the Divine Right of Kings and other such notions.

The Promotion exam supported a hierarchical Great Chain of Being in education. Whether or not children thrive best in groups of similar academic ability is a debate as old as the hills. But where Great Chain thinking failed selective education was when Promotion results determined a child's status for the rest of their career. Once placed in a particular stream, there was little opportunity to be moved up - or indeed down if you subsequently failed to make the grade. This was a major weakness.

Although the Promotion exam (or, it was said, string pulling by influential parents) had placed them in the Academy, there were always a few complete "duds" who really shouldn't have been there. Both the system and these pupils would have benefited from a shift to the High School. Then there were High School pupils who ultimately did much better than some from the Academy. The Promotion exam wasn't a precise enough instrument to place everyone on a specific step of a ladder for their entire school careers. On the other hand some deserving cases might not have particularly welcomed any move up.

The Promotion probably got it right most of the time but couldn't cater for late development and wasn't good enough to exclude the need for subsequent mobility between classes and schools. Even within one school, there were clear anomalies. One of my Dalneigh colleagues must have just squeezed into the Academy since he went into 1D, and ended up with a PhD in Chemistry, just as a member of 1C aspired to a Professorship.

Some received an Academy recommendation but, for various reasons, declined the offer. There were poor families who needed everyone earning a wage as soon as possible. This increased pressure to leave school for employment at 15, so six years of academic education seemed neither practicable nor of much use. Other families just didn't rate the value of education and a few disliked an institution which, not unjustifiably until the 1960s, they saw as snobbish and privileged. And then there were gifted pupils who simply wanted to do Technical, in which the Academy only had non-certificate courses, or Commercial which it didn't do at all.

Anecdotally, it appears that more girls than boys declined the offer of an Academy place and you do have to wonder whether this reflected the last vestiges of the attitude that an academic education was of less relevance to girls?

That was the background to Scotland's entire P7 cohort being herded into rooms of desks (for us it was Dalneigh's GP room) in February 1965 to sit the Promotion exam. We also had an IQ test, 12 months on from a similar one in P6. The Promotion exam was based on the English and Arithmetic curriculum described in the last chapter, so some of the less able pupils must have found it pretty well impossible.

Looking back, the interpretation was pretty stiff. So were the grammar questions and high standards were expected in the composition while the arithmetic required considerable levels of numeracy. The main reason the Promotion exam failed to fine tune selection across the entire ability range was that it was pretty well impossible to set a single exam which could discriminate right across it, identify three secondary streams and subdivide each of them. Even a few years later, almost all primary pupils would have really struggled with an exam like that - not due to lack of ability but because curriculum and methodology changed dramatically.

I never felt any particular pressure sitting the Promotion, but I was never prone to exam stress and sometimes even enjoyed them. I suppose I was pretty confident that I would "make the Academy" and we never thought about allocation to A to D classes. Around three months later, John MacLeod appeared at our classroom door with a piece of foolscap paper in his hand. This was decision time.

He rapidly went through our names, announcing "Academic course at the Academy" or "Technical/Commercial course at the High School" or "General course at the High School". I remember no particular dramatics from anyone, but on the other hand most seemed to get what they expected. One girl, who often finished third in the class, got a Commercial course, presumably by choice. The family owned quite a successful business, so there was clearly no economic pressure.

Around half of the 16 or so who received an academic recommendation went on to gain degrees at a time when university education extended not nearly as far down the ability range as now. For a primary school in a council housing estate, this was reckoned to be pretty good. On the other hand, this was a council estate populated according to 1960s demography, with far more of the professional middle classes than would be found now.

When I began teaching in 1976, I did a study relating First Year Maths marks to pupils' primary schools. There were indeed catchment area differences, but when I performed a similar exercise around 25 years later I found much greater polarisation between schools in private and in council or former council housing areas. This almost certainly reflects the intervening dispersal of professional workers to growing private developments, which was probably only in its early stages by 1976.

Educational selection did create and perpetuate class-based issues. This included the institutional snobbery which was to be found at the Academy, certainly into the 1960s. Its fee paying reputation took time to filter out of social attitudes, especially when fees continued in the primary department until 1961. Conversely, this created some resentment of the place among some "non-Academy" families.

Even after fee paying stopped when the primary department disappeared, social stratification continued for a while. Some staff contrived to perpetuate it by surrogating the perceived superiority of the defunct primary department on former pupils of the very middle class Crown School. Many children who would have attended the fee paying Academy primary, had it survived, now attended Crown instead. It was sometimes also claimed that if you were a doctor's child, you could do no wrong.

In the 1940s Nancy Sutherland, who as Nancy Scott became a hugely popular supply teacher at Dalneigh and then a very successful Head Teacher at Smithton, received her secondary education at the Academy. She was one of a very strong First Year intake from Merkinch Primary and remembered the condescending attitude of a number of Academy staff to what they called "The Merkinch Lot". And then in the 1950s, we find Rector DJ MacDonald expressing expectations in his Log Book that parents would attend the afternoon Prefects' Installation. He does not appear to take much account of how difficult it was in some employments to get a half day's leave, including for working mothers.

Indeed, a number of FPs from the DJ MacDonald era have been more than content to admit that snobbery and elitism were rife. One even went as far as to suggest to me that the Rector himself had a lot to answer for by creating and perpetuating these attitudes. DJ, it has been claimed, wanted to model Inverness Royal Academy along the lines of an English Public School and this was also why rugby was officially promoted much more heavily than football, which was in fact looked down upon.

By 1965 this kind of thing was on its way out and indeed the next Rector, WS Macdonald who took over in 1962, should receive some credit for that. Certainly there was little social apartheid among pupils and a number of my friends, very good ones, lived in private housing. It was only years later that, retrospectively, I became more aware of having been a "Dalneigh Scaff" in this hierarchical establishment and the "Dalneigh Scaffs" didn't do badly either.

In second year, Iain and I took first and third places overall in class 2A. Then in S5, four pupils got six straight A passes in their Highers - the two of us and two Crown FPs. We weren't the first either. In 1963, Joan Cumming and Helen Smith had taken the top two places in 1A and Pamela Beevers joined them to make it a Dalneigh 1-2-3 in English.

There was some historical rivalry, antagonism even, between the Academy and the High School. This went back for decades to when the two schools were just 100 yards apart and High School pupils used some Academy accommodation. When the Academy was in Academy Street until 1895, the rivalry was with the "Bellers" from Bell's School round the corner in Farraline Park. This prompted some vicious battles, including snowball fights.

Some High School pupils resented what they saw as a presumption of superiority by their counterparts. The old rhyme went: "The Caddy Rats take of their hats and bow to the Tecky teachers" or another of several variations thereof. But apart from once being chased home from the Baths, the worst antagonism I ever heard from a High School pupil was "Ach, away home and swot yer Latin!"

There was no shortage of Academy snobbery when the High School started to play rugby in about 1967. The notion of this so called "hooligans' game" being something "played by gentleman" was very much alive and well "up the hill". It also has to be said that the Head of PE Bill Murray was probably at the front of the queue when it came to notions of Academy elitism and superiority - despite having for many years lived in a council house in St Fergus Drive and cycled to school. When these High School "upstarts" presumed to take up this gentlemen's game, they did have scorn poured on them by some at the Academy.

Paradoxically Millburn playing rugby was deemed perfectly acceptable and natural even though, as a Junior Secondary, it was another step further down the educational Chain Of Being. There were one or two factors involved. The Academy's longstanding rivalry was with the High School while Millburn was new, and also had some pupils from residential properties near the Academy. And Colin Baillie taught PE at both schools for some years, which I believe did a lot to create detente between them.

Educational change would soon mean that the High School/Academy educational "Old Firm" would give way to the "New Firm" of the Academy and Millburn. The 1970s reorganisation left them both as comprehensives with adjacent catchment areas, creating a new rivalry. The period of this reorganisation is outwith the scope of this book, but a brief description rounds this chapter off quite nicely.

When a Labour government was elected in 1964, and in 1966 won a majority big enough to see it through to 1970, the writing was on the wall for selective education. Some of Inverness-shire's senior secondary schools, such as Kingussie and Lochaber, were already comprehensives in effect since they were the only schools in their areas. Such schools were often supported by peripheral two or three year secondaries such as at Beauly and Sir E Scott on Harris. This also applied to most other Highlands and Islands institutions such as Dingwall Academy and the Nicholson Institute.

However Inverness itself, due to its size and the existence of selection, was ripe for comprehensive reorganisation and this was a hugely complex process, taking around a decade. It was made all the more difficult by ROSLA, the raising of the school leaving age to 16 in 1972, which created a larger pupil population.

The last Promotion exam was held in 1970 and from 1971 pupils went from primary to their neighbourhood secondary. This was relatively straightforward in west Inverness where the comprehensive intake moved steadily up through the High School and pressure on accommodation was relieved when Charleston Academy appeared in the late 70s.

On the east of the Ness there was a much bigger problem. The only two secondary schools were just half a mile apart so much of the area was local to neither of them. A new school was also needed to serve the expanding Culloden area, but Culloden Academy would not be complete until 1981 and, in the brave new world of comprehensive education, what on earth were they to do with the formerly selective Royal Academy?

For a time in the early 70s there was actually some danger of Inverness Royal Academy disappearing altogether, taking with it almost 200 years of educational history and tradition. Indeed this was actually the aim of some hardline traditionalist former pupils who could not stomach the school's name being sullied by comprehensive status and briefly campaigned for its extinction!

The solution was to build a new comprehensive at Culduthel and, rather than call it something like Slackbuie High, perpetuate the name of Inverness Royal Academy there instead. This gave it a clear geographical catchment area next door to Millburn's while Culloden's would be further east still. However this new building would not be ready until 1977, which resulted in Millburn being packed to the rafters for several years. It would have to hold all First and Second Year pupils for east Inverness until they could be spread across all three proposed comprehensives. In the mid-70s this meant that Millburn had around 550 pupils in 19 classes in each of its two junior years... and extremely packed corridors during period changeovers. At the end of S2, those considered capable of at least one Higher would go to the Academy which hence became a semi-selective secondary catering for S3 to S6. Meanwhile Millburn held on to the others from S3 right through to Fifth Year Leavers (known and not infrequently stigmatised as "ROSLA kids") for the whole of east Inverness.

It took a few years for this plan to work its way through and also to work out of the other end of the Royal Academy after its Culduthel building opened in 1977. Midmills said goodbye to its last Academy pupils in 1979 and then housed the new Culloden Academy for a couple of sessions before being taken over by Inverness College. By 1981, Inverness had completed its transition and was served by five free standing comprehensive schools.

CHAPTER 7 – RELIGION.

By now we have long over-reached our main timescale and need to depart education for a while and look at a different aspect of institutional life in Inverness.

When we came to Inverness in the mid-50s, the short stretch of the river between the Royal Northern Infirmary and the Black Bridge housed no fewer than nine busy churches representing four different denominations. Before long the Methodists, evicted from their Union Street premises by a fire in 1961, built a new church near Friars Shott to augment that ecumenical gathering. Inverness also had plenty others such as St Stephen's, the East, St John's and the Free Presbyterians and most still survive, or just about, mostly with depleted numbers.

However, the Queen Street, St Columba High and West Churches have all since been abandoned by the Church of Scotland in response to falling attendances and changing demographics. As new housing schemes appeared after World War II, the existing churches were supplemented by the likes of Dalneigh and Hilton, but until then the town's religious hub, reflecting its early population distribution, was very much by the riverside.

Since the Reformation, religion in Inverness had been dominated by the Church of Scotland. However there were plenty of other denominations; the Scottish Episcopalians, Roman Catholics, Baptists, Plymouth Brethren and Methodists all had up to three places of worship each. Then, amid a bewildering series of fragmentations following the original Disruption of 1843, various offshoots of the "Free" persuasion proliferated – a consequence of fall outs, usually over the severity of the prevailing brand of Presbyterianism.

In 1989 one of these splinter groups, the Associated Presbyterian Churches, set down its national roots in Inverness. This followed an almighty row among the Free Presbyterians about one of their elders, former Lord Chancellor Lord MacKay of Clashfern, attending a Catholic Requiem Mass for his legal colleague Lord Wheatley.

Church attendance was by no means universal but places of worship were still busy until the mid 20th century marked the swansong for much of organised religion. Once churchgoing became less fashionable and no longer enforceable as in previous centuries by law or by a fear of Hell and Damnation, attendances declined. Meanwhile the Inverness population decentralised to new, peripheral housing areas such as Raigmore, Drakies, Lochardil and Scorguie. Most of the riverside churches emptied steadily and some failed to survive, so the Church of Scotland in particular implemented a process of rationalisation and contraction.

On our arrival in 1956, there was still no shortage of busy, vibrant churches for my parents to choose from. Like many of their generation, they held strong religious beliefs, regularly attended the Church of Scotland and were devout with it. But they were also liberal in their approach and certainly not Sabbatarians, so while they encouraged me to become involved in the church and its organisations, this was by no means a three line whip. The choice was mine and at least twice they cheerfully accepted my decisions to become less involved than I might. Meanwhile the rest of Sundays were mine to enjoy insofar as this was possible in Inverness.

During the period he spent in Inverness before my mum and I moved from Wick, my dad began to attend the Old High Church. However my mother was greatly underwhelmed by its ancient austerity, and equally impressed by St Columba High's warm welcome and much more appealing interior.

This latter feature was born out of extreme misfortune. The church, opened on the junction of Bank Street and Fraser Street in 1843, was burnt to a shell in 1940 and rebuilt inside along very attractive lines. Latterly, restored cinema seats replaced hard pews thanks to one of the congregation, Provost Robert Wotherspoon, who was a director of Caledonian Associated Cinemas. Ultimately my mother's view prevailed and St Columba High it was.

The latter history of St Columba High partly mirrors that of its parent body the Church of Scotland. When we started going there, the place was packed. I actually found my first visits, aged 3, quite overwhelming especially when this dense throng of people began to sing very loudly. The church became so packed that a balcony had to be added and services had to take place in the church hall for several months as work progressed. It would not be required for long.

St Columba was also quite a wealthy church, as I soon discovered after a few occasions watching my dad and his colleagues count the collection. The congregation was not short of quite prominent members of the community. Apart from Provost Wotherspoon there was the legendary Miss Eveline Barron, Editor and Proprietor of The Inverness Courier. Then there were John and Ruth Edgar representing two local business dynasties – he the thriving baker's in Church Street and she Smith's the up market outfitters round the corner in Queensgate. And there were several more who weren't short of funds either.

Churches, however wealthy, never seem to be backward at coming forward in pursuit of more money. When I was about 10 they decided to hold a "Stewardship Campaign" to boost what was known as the "Freewill Offering". A cynic might suggest that these euphemisms were some kind of cover for a form of extortion involving blackmail of a moral variety. That was especially true of the "Blessing Boxes". The idea there was that if you experienced something that made you feel "blessed", such as recovery from illness or the safe return of a loved one, you put money into the box. I dismissed this simply as the retrospective purchase of good fortune and an especially devious means of getting cash out of people. I always wondered if football pools winners were expected to place a slice of their gains in their Blessing Box?

The minister's stipend at St Columba was well above the going rate and on that one, my mother used to make a very perceptive observation on the appointment of clergy: "The Lord never seems to call them to where there isn't a bigger stipend." Apart from collections, people were always leaving bequests and legacies to St Columba High. This wealth led to the theory that Church of Scotland HQ's decision to close the place in the 2000s had certain elements of an asset stripping exercise.

Until my dad got a car in the early 60s, we would frequently walk to Church - a longer trek from Dalneigh than from Kenneth Street. On the way home we would often get a lift from Duncan

Chisholm the kiltmaker who lived in Columba Road. Other times it might be Bill Anderson who used to own the baker's shop at the top of Academy Street and whose family also used to run the Catch My Pal temperance organisation. His wife and daughter, both Minnie, were good friends of my mother and Bill would take a diversion via St Andrew Drive on his way home to Crown Circus. The real leather seats in his Rover 100 exuded an aroma of class.

One of the good things about St Columba High was the relative lack of self-righteousness and zealotry about the people who went there. Most were thoroughly decent folk, true in their belief but genuine, cordial and sociable with it. Holy Willies were pretty few and far between. Holy Willyism, satirised brilliantly by Robert Burns, is a more general aspect of Christianity that I did begin to look upon with increasing distaste. However the more recent decline of religion has left a vacuum in society in the area of self-righteous, holier and thou, coercive behaviour. This has largely been filled instead by Political Correctness obsessives and the claustrophobic sanctimony of "Wokery".

It would be some time before I regularly experienced the extensive rigours of a full sermon. When we started going there I was just old enough to attend the Sunday School which exited the church en masse after a couple of hymns and a prayer, also waiting for any baptisms.

Head of the infants' Sunday School in the lower Dr Black Memorial Hall was a wonderful lady called Elizabeth - or Betty - Chalmers. Betty had come to Inverness from Edinburgh in 1937 to teach infants at Inverness Royal Academy but married in 1939, which then obliged women to leave teaching. She became a

Sunday School teacher at St Columba High, and continued for over half a century. One of her anecdotes was how, on September 3rd 1939, she was attending the Sunday service and John Edgar left to go and listen to Neville Chamberlain's 11:15 broadcast on his car radio. A few minutes later he returned and had a quiet word with the Minister, the Rev Ernest Elliott, who duly told the congregation that Britain was at war with Germany.

Betty Chalmers had a very special way with very young children, as many who attended her Kindergarten in Ballifeary Road also found out. She was kindly but firm and little ones, including myself, just took naturally to her and ate out of her hand. It was a sad day when I had to leave her little Sunday School and go upstairs to the senior one.

There were two annual social rituals – the Sunday School Party and the Sunday School Picnic. The former, at Christmas, comprised an obscene exhibition of gluttony far outstripping any of the other six Deadly Sins, bookended by party games and films on an old fashioned reel to reel projector. Then in June, everyone would pile on to a bus to be driven to the Balgate shinty ground at Kiltarlity for a feast of outdoor activities and a somewhat less gluttonous refuelling.

I now look on education in religion quite critically – cynically almost – since too often it amounts to indoctrination. Presenting matters of faith via an implication of fact gives the message a massive head start in the minds of young children before they develop critical faculties to evaluate what they are being told. Religion's historical keenness to become involved in education perhaps has more of a self serving side to it than meets the eye. However my parents didn't send me to Sunday School to have me indoctrinated. It was simply "what one did" and religion was something that was never really directly talked about at home, although there we often spoke about the church which was a big part of our social lives.

They very much left me to adopt my own religious values over time. Through to my early 20s these, if anything, intensified of my own volition before very gradually declining for the next quarter century. By that point I had adopted my own personal theology which didn't involve the collectivism of church attendance. However the final straw was the minister's complete neglect of my mother during the months before she died in 2000, after more than 40 years' service to that church. I never crossed its threshold after that.

There was certainly no "Bible bashing" at home and Bibles were not carried to church. I think my parents looked on that as an unnecessary manifestation of self-righteousness and virtue signalling. We did say Grace ("Thank you for the world so sweet thank you for the food we eat....") but active religion played no part in daily family life.

In 1967, aged 14, it was time to move up again to the Bible Class. This was a whole different ball game since, instead of leaving after about 20 or 30 minutes, its members were expected to sit through the entire service before going to the church hall until 1pm. Along with some others, I also attended Boys' Brigade Bible Class from 10 until church started at 11, so this was going to mean three solid hours of religion in three different settings.

So I said "No", and my parents agreed with me. I did do the decent thing and wrote to the minister, Rev

Stephen Frew, who held the charge from 1953 until 1975, to tell him of my decision. However I must admit that stressing pressures of homework ahead of my straightforward unwillingness to do three solid hours of religion was a bit disingenuous.

The effect was unexpected to say the least. Stephen Frew, possibly unaware that my extreme reluctance to sit through his sermons partly drove my initiative, immediately instituted changes. These saw the Bible Class also leave the church, although slightly later than the Sunday School - indeed just before that dreaded sermon! He admitted privately that this was "a knot that needed cut" and was pleased that I had given him the opportunity to cut it.

Sermons are probably the aspect of church services which are more of a turn off than any other. Too many ministers forget that their congregations don't have a degree in theology and have no real interest in the more obscure and erudite aspects of the Christian faith. They just want to get on with their lives according to its principles. Very rare indeed are sermons which I did not contemplate with dread and endure amid the abiding hope of the dentist's chair that it would all be over sooner rather than later. Latterly, I developed the skill of falling asleep without obviously doing so and waking to the first organ chord of the final hymn.

I've always reckoned that if, despite an extensive education, I hadn't a clue what they were going on about, then what chance had the average person in the pew? Half an hour of boring the backside off people does little to promote motivation and, in retrospect, it seems strange that I persisted for so long with a Sunday morning activity, the central part of which never had any appeal to me at all. My mother used to reckon that ministers just couldn't resist a captive audience. I think she was right but, with congregations no longer coerced by the threat of the penitent stool, the clergy failed to realise that the audience wasn't nearly as captive as it used to be.

Stephen Frew, despite many endearing characteristics, used to deliver sermons of up to that half hour. His successor at St Columba was Alastair Younger who would relieve the congregation of a similar part of their lives that they would never get back, but with far fewer words. If I'd had access to compact and discreet modern recording technology it would have been revealing to record one of his sermons, edit out only the pretentious and presumptuous pregnant pauses, but no words, and play it back to him at about one third of its original length.

The Bible Class leader was Ruth Edgar whose family home was The Tilt on Old Perth Road which we also used to visit for social evenings. "Ruthie" really was far too nice for her own good, unfortunately to the extent of extreme naivety. I often wondered if she believed that her entire group of 14-18 year olds subscribed to exactly the same utterly well meaning and scrupulously Christian practices and values as she did?

For instance one of her favourite teaching aids was called "The Teen Commandments", designed to instil clean and orderly living into adolescents. These included the slogan "Beer is best - left alone" which she declared time and again.... blissfully unaware that some of her older charges were sitting there nursing mild hangovers from the previous evening's conviviality.

154

For me, one of the highlights of the Sunday morning services, and occasional evening ones I attended, were the organ voluntaries played at each end. Beforehand it might be something more tranquil like Mascagni's intermezzo from Cavalleria Rusticana but afterwards you could expect an altogether more rousing rendition like Handel's Arrival of the Queen of Sheba.

St Columba was very lucky with its organists and my time began with Jimmy MacAdam, the County Music Organiser. Later there was David Hardie, one of Inverness's best known musical figures, who wasn't averse to nipping round to the Cummings Hotel for a dram during the minister's evening sermon. He is well remembered for using his key to the Church Hall not altogether discreetly and for founding the Sine Nomine Singers, the pronunciation of whose name used to cause frequent problems.

One time David got thoroughly drunk and phoned the minister who couldn't understand how his incoherent babblings could have been induced by the "Orangey" he kept going on about. The full title of "Glenmorangie" might have helped. And then there was Millburn's Head of Music, Tom Anderson, who would do a shift with the Tenerife Trio in the Caley Hotel on the Saturday night, go home to sleep and come back down for the Sunday morning service almost next door.

Another thriving institution at St Columba High was the 1st Inverness Company of the Boys' Brigade. The BB was founded in 1883 by Thurso man Sir William Alexander Smith and soon flourished. In the 1960s, the 12 town companies of the Inverness Battalion played a formidable role in community life and probably outnumbered the rival Boy Scouts.

I have always found these two institutions intriguing, especially when you compare them. By the time I left the BB in 1971, I had reached the view that both organisations were instruments of compliance, but only the BB extended that to religion in any great way, while the Scouts were more secular.

The BB was also run on military lines, many of them quite anachronistic. The uniform comprised a late Victorian army pillbox hat, leather belt and white haversack - all items which required very high maintenance. Meanwhile the military drill was what would have organised soldiers into lines and squares at Waterloo and was already obsolescent come the First World War. The hierarchy was strictly along army lines. Boys (always with a capital "B") ranged from Private to Staff Sergeant and officers - Lieutenants and Captains - oversaw Companies which were subdivided into Squads and aggregated into Battalions.

The BB Object sums up its standpoint rather well: "The advancement of Christ's Kingdom among boys and the promotion of habits of Obedience, Reverence, Discipline and Self Respect and all that tends towards a true Christian manliness". In many ways this was a metaphor for the then moribund British Empire – conquered and controlled by military strength under an umbrella of evangelistic Christianity.

And while the BB thought its troops were still guarding that Empire, the Scouts seemed to believe that they were still ruling it! A list of outmoded ranks such as Patrol Leader and District Commissioner - straight out of the Raj - oversaw a world of woggles, dustbin lid hats and bizarre Boer War practices such as fieldcraft and living off the land. You half expected Sanders of the River to arrive to relieve Mafeking in a canoe paddled by a group of natives. Devotion to The Queen was possibly even more fervent in the Scouts than the BB, but both organisations lived partly in a bygone age. And as the British Empire was rapidly dismantled and Britain ceased to be a superpower, both became increasingly incongruous.

Boys' Brigade Queen's Badge presentation, May 1969. Front - James Gordon, myself. Rear - Cameron Stuart, Eddie Riach, Dougie Riach.

I was destined for BB membership since my dad was a committed Boys' Brigade man. He had been a

157

member of the 1st Wick Company until the war and, on moving south, became a Lieutenant in St Columba's 1st Inverness before aspiring to the Captaincy. In 1960 I joined the Life Boys as the BB's younger wing was called before it became the Junior Section. And just as the main BB was army based, the Life Boys were decidedly naval. The uniform was navy blue, traditional sailors' hats were worn and Leading Boys (as opposed to Leading Seamen) wore lanyards, while female officers had Nelsonian three cornered hats. The overarching BB emblem, an anchor, which also inspired its motto - Sure and Stedfast (sic) - was also naval and the BB hymn was Will Your Anchor Hold in the Storms of Life.

The Life Boy leader was Miss Ishbel Crawford who, like Mrs Chalmers, had a great way with younger children. Quite late in life she married one of the Town Officers, Charlie Rose, who had been widowed. Also playing a big part in that Life Boy team was George MacKintosh who could probably lay claim to being Inverness's "Mr BB". George, who came from a well off family, lived on Leys Drive, never seemed to work and spent much of his time on Boys' Brigade business. He was our group's pianist and while the Life Boys didn't do formal army drill, we did get "maze marching" round the hall to George rattling out Elgar's Pomp and Circumstance March Number 4.

The group met at 7pm on a Friday in the lower church hall for a range of more recreational activities and the inevitable football. This included the ritual of an inspection where one of the leaders would pass along a row of boys who in turn would hold out his hands, both palms and backs, and then raise each knee so their cleanliness – which was clearly next to

Godliness – could also be verified.

A small number of older Life Boys had already graduated to long trousers but, bizarrely, still lifted both knees for inspection! One unfortunate consequence of this inspection was that just before leaving the house on a Friday night, there would be a thorough scrubbing of my knees by my mother. This wasn't the only knee washing of the week, but it was certainly the most rigorous and it was a sensation which I absolutely hated.

Transition to the BB company, which met upstairs at 7:45 after the Girl Guides had finished there, came on starting secondary school. At this point I still accepted the BB Modus Operandi uncritically. This was, after all, in the genes but as I progressed through secondary school, I began increasingly to question the military aspects, such as the completely outdated drill and uniforms. This just seemed so utterly pointless, although apologists would argue that the BB instilled discipline. That worked just too well for me at one Battalion Parade in the Merkinch Church when the minister said "Stand up" and I instantly did as instructed. It took me a couple of seconds to realise that he was just announcing the hymn "Stand up, stand up for Jesus" and here I was alone on my feet, red faced among hundreds of still sedentary boys.

"Tallest on the right, shortest on the left - in single rank.... size!"..... "Company... Kumpanay!.... attenSHUN!"...... "Left turn, right wheel, about turn". What on earth was the point of all this stuff which you even had to pass an exam in before you could get your Queen's Badge?

Lamont Graham, another BB legend, captain of the 5th, East Church company and Battalion

Adjutant, also had a further command all of his own. Once a year, we had a Battalion Church Parade and initially assembled in the Washington Court BB hall, demolished in the late 70s to make way for Marks and Spencer. And "Scoobies", as he was universally known, would inevitably bring the parade to proper order with the command "Stop gu'ereen!" (which is Parliamo Inverness for "guttering" or fidgeting.) Latterly on Church Parades I even took to expressing my dissent by marching with my hands in my pockets.

But there was a lot more to the BB than drill, which usually followed the 7:45 Inspection of 30 or so Boys in four squads. Here the shine on belts and the blanco on haversacks and pillboxes would be religiously scrutinised by officers who, across the organisation at that time, included not a few World War II ex-servicemen. It was possibly due to these men, for whom drill and "bulling" of uniforms had been a way of life for years, that the military ethos lasted as long as it did.

From 7pm there were various classes for small groups, aimed at gaining badges such as Signaller's (when Morse Code was still alive and well), Arts and Crafts and Fireman's, most of them right through to Advanced Certificates. There was also preparation for the Duke of Edinburgh's awards and the prestigious Queen's Badge.

Most memorable of all for me was the First Aid badge where I found the classes, run by a local pharmacist called Sandy Gray, absolutely fascinating. Sandy did all the basic bandaging and so on, but also covered a lot of human anatomy. Sandy's anatomy lessons, such as on the structure of the heart and lungs, were the foundations on which I laid enough physiology and biochemistry to provide the theory behind my athletics coaching.

Drill was followed by PT when the company's "horse" was trundled out. These wooden sections with a leather top and a springboard were a staple part of gym work and one big achievement was to do the "splits" lengthwise over the thing.

The Battalion also held drill and PT competitions plus the battalion sports and cross country races. The athletics convener was Walter Banks who was another of our company's officers and these competitions were meat and drink to me. However I never got an overall award since, although a regular winner of the 100, the 220 and the half mile, I just couldn't jump.

Friday evenings always ended with that BB staple, indoor football in the upper hall. The organisation was a great breeding ground for young Inverness players and Jackie Sutherland, Captain of the 7th (Queen Street) and later the 10th (Methodist) companies and John Beaton, who joined Jackie after an upbringing in the 12th (Dalneigh), were for decades among the town's most prominent youth coaches.

Many fine players came through Inverness BB ranks. Kevin MacDonald was in the 5th East Church Company, as was Billy Urquhart who sandwiched periods with Rangers and Wigan between extensive spells at Caley, for whom he scored the last competitive goal at Telford Street Park in 1994. Meanwhile the name of Billy's great friend and rival Davie Milroy of the 9th Hilton was synonymous with Inverness Thistle. In the early 1970s, all three were BB Boys together with Billy and Kevin 5th Company colleagues. My own extreme lack of footballing talent meant that when it came to inter-company games, I was usually at best the First Reserve - as often as not "non-playing".

My dad took over the Captaincy from Alastair Tulloch who in turn had succeeded Peter MacGregor. Other officers at the time, apart from Walter Banks, included Jimmy Halley and Robert Hunter and it was certainly a friendly company. I retained connections with some of the other lads for years to come. For instance I saw a great deal of Dougie Riach when he was a Thistle committee man during the Inverness football merger and I would frequently bump into John McBean on a Saturday night in the Legion, often when I was in the company of John "Jud" Douglas of the 7th.

Because my dad was one of them, I was aware of further great camaraderie among the Inverness Battalion's officers. Apart from Scoobies, Jackie Sutherland and John Beaton, these included ex-Highland League footballer Rodwill Clyne at the 9th, the long serving Peter Home at the 4th (Old High), and Ian Reid at the 2nd (Ness Bank). Alec Howie was captain of the 12th (Dalneigh), Bill MacDonald of the 8th (West Church) and a gentleman by the name of MacLeod at the 4th Company was so short sighted that he went under the nickname "Teetums".

The big annual BB event was the Battalion Camp at its permanent site at Carrbridge. Dozens of boys would pile on to buses which would go down the A9, up Drumossie Brae, through the Moy bends and over the Slochd where the German's Head would be pointed out in the rock face to the uninitiated. On arrival at the campsite at the eastern edge of the village we would be greeted by the Advance Party who had already put up the L-shaped arrangement of sleeping tents. Officers slept along the base and boys up the side, while beside the huts which served as a kitchen and canteen, there was a marquee which was the mess, plus a bell tent for the cooks, Rod and Hugh.

They served up great food, although breakfast came with something of a hangover for them since they enjoyed their evenings in the local pub. My dad was camp Quartermaster and one of his jobs was to operate the tuck shop at the end of one of the huts. There was usually great demand at the end of a day of swimming, canoeing, expeditions, sports and non-stop activity.

In 1969, the 6th Company managed to get just a little further than Carrbridge. In the best traditions of the Cliff Richard film Summer Holiday, they all piled on a bus and headed for a company trip to Italy which is still spoken about among Merkinch BB veterans.

By the time I got to Sixth Year in school, my enthusiasm for the BB had waned, despite having won the Queens Badge and aspired to the rank of Sergeant. Many of the activities were less relevant to me and while my dad knew this, I also felt a degree of loyalty and the need to support him. We therefore came to a deal that I would attend the BB (and chat up the Girl Guides on their way out) until the parade was over and then I was free to slip away to meet my pals or a girlfriend or whatever.

With Boys' Brigade, Life Boys, Girl Guides and Brownies, St Columba's uniformed youth organisations were very active at a time when there was no shortage of similar activities. Ness Bank Church was one which had a company of the Girls' Brigade, also a church based organisation. There were also Sea Scouts around and others of more military origins such as the Army Cadets and Air Training Corps. They all joined together on Armistice Sunday to parade to Cavell Gardens along with local dignitaries and, most important of all, veterans who were still plentiful in numbers, including not a few from World War 1.

On Sunday nights, St Columba had a very lively youth group called Meeting Point. Run by Gerald Fraser, it was an informal blend of games, discussions and talks, with little or no Bible Bashing. As such it reflected the quite liberal attitude within St Columba High to Sunday activity. One Sunday night I walked home via Fairfield Road with Mary Anderson and she invited me in for coffee. This was with some trepidation since her father was Bill Anderson, Head Teacher at the High School, who had a reputation as something of a hard man. My concerns were totally groundless and he was as cordial as he was five years later when I did an enjoyable teaching practice at the High School. In the mid-70s, Bill Anderson became a legend among Inverness teachers with a famous prize giving broadside against Highland Regional Council.

The church also gave an extremely professional Nativity Play, produced by Miss Marion Munro who was a leading light in Inverness drama and a well known elocution teacher with a studio in Castle Street. With Marion, who lived with her sister on Diriebught Road, there were no half measures for the cast which was mainly from the Sunday School. She held afternoon rehearsals in the hall on eight Sundays before the performance in the Church on the Sunday night before Christmas. This was preceded by an afternoon dress rehearsal in the

Church itself which was transformed into a theatre, with The Angel Gabriel emerging from the organ loft. This meant that in November and December, some of us would be at the church or the halls in the morning for two Bible Classes and the service, in the afternoon for a play rehearsal and back again in the evening for Meeting Point.

Costumes were hired from Moultries of Edinburgh and every move and word were made perfect by Marion. Proper stage make up was also used and my mother used to dread when I was cast as the Black King, heavily made up and returning home with badly marked clothes and a dirty face. And I do wonder what modern day Disciples of Woke would make of children performing in a Christian pageant and "blacking up" for the purpose?! One day, a Snowflake will find out about this and exact revenge by pulling down a statue of me.

The theatrically gifted Chisholm family belonged to our church and often took part. Jimmy senior, a renowned local drama performer, made a fearsome Herod many years before Jimmy junior moved on to the heights of Wishee Washee in the Inverness pantomime and Jimmy Blair in Take the High Road.

One cornerstone of many Church of Scotland congregations was the Women's Guild, a formidable assembly of ladies often presided over by the Minister's wife. This was the arrangement at St Columba High where Betty Frew, an affable and very sociable lady who was also mother to five unusually tall children, was in benevolent charge. Alan, her youngest, was in Sixth Year when I entered the Academy and one of the older girls married Mrs Chalmers' son Murray who became a minister in Edinburgh.

The Guild also did a lot of practical good in the congregation such as supporting older members, or "The Auld" as my mother's friend Mary Banks called them. This was Christianity in action if you like. The congregation's other gestures of practical humanity included distributing to disadvantaged children and the elderly, gifts of toys and produce taken by the Sunday School to the Christmas and Harvest Thanksgiving services.

St Columba High Church was a building where I used to feel especially comfortable (not just because of the cinema seats), secure and at peace. Its most prominent features were its elaborate rose window, large communion table and a pulpit with a lectern cloth bearing the emblem and motto of the Church of Scotland. This comes from the story in Genesis of Moses and the Burning Bush and the cloth carried an image of that, with the words "Nec Tamen Consumebatur". Once we got to Latin verbs in the Passive Voice in around Third Year, I was able to translate this myself as "And yet it was not consumed".

St Columba High became such a central part of my social life that, even after I went to university, I maintained ongoing ties, which included coming off the train on a weekend home from Edinburgh and heading straight to the church hall to meet friends attending Guides and BB.

Over the years, though, there have been great changes to church life in Inverness and everywhere else and indeed I am one of the many who put church going aside across that intervening period.

CHAPTER 8 - CADDY RATS.

The former Inverness Royal Academy at Midmills - phase 1 dating from 1895.

I know this because I did it myself a year later. Kids who have just finished First Year at secondary school, out of sheer devilment, just love to wind up their fellows who are about to join them from primary; and so it was in that summer of 1965. Irrespective of whether you were heading for the High School or to become a Caddy Rat at the Academy, there was always someone there to put the fear of death into you with all manner of stories - overwhelmingly fabrications.

Those heading for Montague Row were regaled with the idiosyncrasies of The Beast and the anomalies of Tubby Telford whilst being well warned about how handy Garden in the Tecky Department was with the belt. Meanwhile others headed up Stephen's Brae in trepidation at the thought of Jess Thomson's unpredictable explosions, the alleged ferocity of Duggie and still with a lingering doubt about whether Fritz really was a homicidal former SS Sergeant.

But when we got to the Academy, it fairly soon became apparent that these accounts had been greatly exaggerated and that eccentricity was a far more prevalent among the staff than ferocity ever was. Similarly, it turned out that Fingals, Murphy and Percy were simply harmless Second Year worthies who wouldn't hurt a fly.

Most of the Dalneigh squad who were Academy bound ended up on the same town bus on that late August morning in 1965 and we all walked up the brae together. Past the Plough, Greenwalds the Bookies and the large advertising hoardings – onwards and upwards on a journey which, up or down, many would make around 2000 times over the next six years – more if you were one of the many who still went home for "dinner".

What we found was a building which had evolved in four phases. The front section, dating from 1895, comprised 17 classrooms, two offices and the library which had formerly been the assembly hall. Behind that on one side was an extension opened in 1913 with a boys' gym and 12 classrooms, including science and art accommodation. Parallel with it and separated by the Quad was what had begun life as the Primary department. As this was phased out from the mid-1950s, these areas had become rooms for "cookery", administration, girl prefects and a girls' gym. Then, completing the fourth side of the Quad, there was a further extension just dating from 1961 with a huge assembly hall, a dining room, physics and woodwork rooms, and then history and geography classes on the first floor.

It was when we were ushered into that assembly

hall with three huge plate glass windows that we made our first error of identity. The man in the blue suit hanging around in front of the stage wasn't after all WS Macdonald the Rector, known universally as Willie Fatlips, but Alec Munro the Janitor. At the end of that first assembly we were allocated our various classes and, as members of 1A, Iain and I joined almost 40 others in Room 25 with Miss Kate MacKenzie our form teacher.

It seems to have been a strange Royal Academy ritual that everyone had to be asked to state publicly their "father's occupation" - always the father's. The particular relevance of this has never been clear and nowadays guidance staff would have elicited that information, if it was considered vital, as part of extensive primary – secondary liaison arrangements. This anachronistic practice also took no account of the possibility that a father might be unemployed. Admitting to this in front of 40 fellows that a child had never met until a few minutes previously would have been highly embarrassing.

One girl, however, killed the process stone dead when it came to her turn and she boldly and bravely intoned: "My father is dead!". This was just one part of an extremely poor set of arrangements for easing the transition from primary to secondary. You were just dumped in at the deep end.

From there it was into our first eight period day. On Mondays, Wednesdays and Fridays assembly lasted from 9 am until 9:10 while on Tuesdays and Thursdays there were 20 minutes with your form teacher for Religious Instruction. The very term smacks of the "intrusion" (thrusting in) of which Muriel Spark's Miss Jean Brodie accused her colleagues, rather than "education" (a leading out).

Religious Education and specialist teachers of that subject were still some years away. There was no room for debate here in schools, where even Roman Catholics could be looked on as virtual heretics.

Period 1 ended at 9:50 and two further 40 minute periods took you to Interval from 11:10 to 11:25. Two more spanned the time until lunch at 12:45 and the break was 75 minutes to allow people time to go home, which many with non-working mothers did. The afternoon then comprised three further 40 minute periods until 4pm.

Getting out of assembly at 9:10 could be something of a crush and to alleviate this, a row of prefects stood down the corridor outside the hall to separate flows of humanity going in opposite directions along it. This was indeed a Thin Blue (and Yellow) Line and it wasn't unknown for the odd fly kick to be aimed at a prefect who had perhaps given somebody detention or a 500 word essay for latecoming. The other morning ritual was in the Quad where the Janitors had placed several metal crates of third of a pint bottles of milk from which pupils who wanted it helped themselves.

The mid-60s janitorial staff were a stark contrast. On the one hand there was the hugely popular Head Janitor of almost 20 years, Alec Munro, who ran the tightest of ships and with a great sense of humour which delighted staff and pupils alike. Alec had a phenomenal repertoire of stories, including not a few about the Rector who, despite a string of degrees and war decorations and having been a former captain of Scotland's amateur football team, could at times be naive in the extreme.

According to Alec, when they did inspections of the school, the Rector would ask questions like "Who is this boy Fatlips that they keep writing about on the walls?". Then on a tour of the Sixth Year boys' toilets, he sniffed the air and said: "Mr Munro.... you've been smoking in here!". And when Alec explained the real source of the smell, the response apparently was: "Well Mr Munro, we'll have to nip this kind of thing in the bud."

Alec's assistant was named Roderick Chisholm, but very few people knew that, because he was never called anything other than Oddjob. This partly reflected his function in the school and partly his strong resemblance to the character in the James Bond film Goldfinger. Oddjob would spend some lunch hours waddling about the place repeatedly intoning "Gerrout....SIDE!" - and absolutely nothing else. If you attempted to remonstrate with him he would just repeat it more loudly – and yet again if you "Gorrout...SIDE" but came back in by another door and he spotted you a second time. Oddjob's alternative lunch time activity was to waddle down Stephen's Brae and pop into Greenwald's the bookies before continuing to one or more of the Eastgate pubs. An invariably less straight line course back up the hill would then involve another foray into Greenwald's to see if he had won anything.

I did steadily develop an entirely new circle of friends in 1A, but from other primary schools and this circle proved to be considerably longer lasting than the much valued associations of Dalneigh. Indeed the group of four that emerged from late 1965 then, at Edinburgh University in the early 70s, became the nucleus of an even wider network from Inverness and beyond which was to last for decades.

Allan MacLeod was never known as anything other than Stan. This had followed him from Crown

School where Allan had soon become Stalin which was quickly corrupted to Stanley and abbreviated to Stan. We had actually met once before. The 1965 Primary Road Safety Quiz had been a head to head for the title between Dalneigh and Crown and Stan was in the Crown team. Stan's voice has always been pretty audible and was very deep even before it broke. At one point he said something rather grotesquely loud into the microphone which was being passed round and had the whole place in stitches.

Stan's own description of himself was "a copper's kid". His dad, Alec MacLeod, was the desk constable at the Police Station in the front corner of the old Bell's School in Farraline Park. The family had one of the police houses on the angle of Old Mill Road and Damfield Road so Stan went to Crown Primary and was one of the first people Iain and I became friendly with.

The other was Richard Smith who had been at Bishop Eden's, just round the corner from where he lived in Huntly Street before the family moved to Kilmuir Road. It was when we shared a double desk in Latin that I got to know Richard well and the four of us gelled quite quickly into a long-lasting quadrumvirate.

We found we had a number of things in common. Academically, all four of us were pretty high fliers and were habitually in the leading group in most subjects in 1A and thereafter. Stan went on to do a PhD in Maths and Richard became a much respected GP in Inverness. We also came from similar backgrounds since none of our families owned their own home. There was also no history of university education among previous generations who grew up at a time when this was a very restricted field.

There was, eventually, a strong sporting link too, but less so in Iain's case. Richard, Stan and I – after my Damascene conversion to sport - all became members of school athletics and rugby teams although Iain's involvement didn't really progress past the Second Year rugby XV. A decade later, we would all have degrees from Edinburgh University, having spent much of our time there in the same accommodation.

We were also very friendly with Stewart Donald who joined us from time to time. Stewart, frequently known as "Stewie", lived in Heatherly Crescent and his dad was a vet at Drummond Hill College of Agriculture. He was a great big fellow from an early age and, as such, a very successful rugby forward. He was also a very decent long distance runner and might have taken that quite a long way had the size of his frame not presented a limiting factor.

With so many of my early friends having moved out of Inverness long since, Stewart is the only one from that era that I still bump into, not infrequently at parkruns and other events since he, like me, still likes to continue to run.

The big novelty of First Year was moving about from one class to another every 40 minutes during an eight period day when we might also see half a dozen different teachers. French and Latin were completely new subjects, as was Technical, otherwise called woodwork, with the hilarious Allan Beattie. When Beattie, in his marked Aberdeen accent, would call "Everyone round the front bench" you knew you were going to be entertained by a man who certainly knew how to get 13 year old boys into stitches.

It was never "wood" - always "material", and

indeed the only time he ever used the former term was in his famous catch phrase "wood doesn't grow on trees, laddie". Then there were other gems such as "hey ho neddie" and "rhubarb and bananas" which kept the pre-adolescent sense of humour fired up. "Tecky" was, however, as strict a preserve of boys as Home Economics (also known as Domestic Science or Cooking) with Miss Rose was for the girls, and so it would remain for some years to come.

I very quickly gained an enthusiasm for Physics with Maude Anderson, a large eccentric and well meaning lady who called everyone, including the Rector, "dearie". Some boys used to hold competitions to see who could utter an obscenity loudest in class without her realising what was being said. Maude joined the Royal Academy staff on August 29th 1939 and it was said that Hitler's desperate response was to invade Poland three days later.

The former Miss Yule had three ambitions in life – a fur coat, a car and a man – and she achieved them all. The fur coat was worn regularly to church; the car, a Hillman Minx in our day, was driven everywhere seemingly in second gear and at 18 mph; and the man – Ian Anderson – was said to have been encountered when he came to do a job in her house. During the school day she would keep her two small dogs in the back of the car and they would invariably yap hysterically at anyone passing. We once slid past and realised that the dogs were asleep, so we gathered in a circle round the car and, on a count of three, all started yapping furiously ourselves. The dogs went berserk and never seemed to bother us quite so much after that.

Physics was one of several subjects where we

found ourselves right at the cutting edge of reforms – the Alternative Syllabi. New courses in the sciences gave rise to new textbooks – Chemistry Takes Shape and Jardine's Physics Is Fun. Not a few copies of the latter had the final word of their titles amended in pen in such a way as to disagree strongly with the assertion being made in it! Both books had the same fundamental weakness – they told you very little on the assumption that you would find it out for yourself from scratch. Fortunately, Maude and our Chemistry teacher Pete Higgins made sure all was explained thoroughly, in Maude's case through reams of handwritten notes reinforced by sticky canvas rings and kept in a green ringbinder.

Modern Maths for Schools with its brightly coloured textbooks, Venn Diagrams and Set Theory was introduced to 1A and 1C that year. It was initially quite different from the "traditional" maths still given to 1B and 1D. But come Higher, we could all (in theory) differentiate, integrate, state the Sine Rule and define the centre of a circle. Only 1A were given a brand new audio-visual French course for the first term, involving slides and tapes - "Nicole a perdu son stylo..... Nicole a perdu son stylo", always repeated like wartime code messages to the French Resistance. And then there were our History for Young Scots textbooks, written by the Academy's Head of Department Sandy Cameron. Although we had notoriously fierce Miss Spence (later Mrs MacKenzie) in First Year, we had the man himself thereafter and he was wonderful.

There was also a modernised textbook for the completely new subject of Latin. It was entitled The Approach To Latin but, as with Physics Is Fun, this was easily corrupted by idle hands to The Approach

To Eating. By this time, although Greek had largely disappeared from the curriculum, Latin still had a few years before it encountered a decline as inexorable as that of the Roman Empire. Only the two top classes got Latin and 1B drew the short straw of the upredictabilities and eccentricities of Jess Thomson. Meanwhile we got her complete antithesis in Sheena Osler, who became Sheena Matheson when we were in Second Year. What I mean by antithesis is that you would never have found Jess in a short skirt and makeup or with a very trendy beehive hairstyle which a number of the younger women teachers adopted.

When Sheena came into the room, she would always declare:"Salvete dscipuli" (greetings, pupils) to which we were required to chorus: "Salve magistra" (greetings teacher). It's a corruption of this Latin greeting of "salve/salvete" that emerges in Frankie Howerd's "salute" welcome in Up Pompeii.

It all started with "amo, amas amat..." and "mensa, mensa, mensam....". Now even though it was a straightforward noun of the First Declension, I could never understand why they started with "mensa". At this point the six cases – nominative, vocative, accusative, genitive, dative and ablative – all had to be taught as well. It was therefore a bit confusing being introduced to the vocative case as something which meant "O, table". Who would want to address a lump of wood? Apart from Allan Beattie.

The complexity of Latin steadily increased through various conjugations and declensions, deponent and semi-deponent verbs, ablatives absolute and the kalends, ides and nones of the various months. By about Third Year we got on to Caesar's Gallic Wars which practice led to us being able to read fluently, and in the end "O" Grade turned out to be quite straightforward. Higher Latin was rather different and three weeks into the course, the Rector made a sudden decision to put a limit of six Highers on any one pupil. Several of us had started seven and most dropped Latin – to the absolute consternation of its Head, Depute Rector David Thom.

Notwithstanding the Alternative courses, this was still a very traditional education largely delivered very formally by traditionally minded but often very, in my experience, good teachers. As we got to know the building and how the school worked, we gradually became more confident, although still in awe of what seemed to us to be huge Adonises and Brunhildes with yellow braid on their blazers, who were the prefects.

Second Year was very much the same as First with the same subjects and largely the same teachers. One change was that in Geography we moved from Bonzo MacKintosh in Room 33 through to Jimmy Johnstone, known widely as Abdul, in 34. When David Thom died suddenly late in 1970, Jimmy became Depute Rector until he retired in 1989 and was known for his conspicuous bow tie and spontaneous irascibility if provoked.

Sometimes, when along the corridor in History, you would hear Abdul's door open and close, followed immediately by this high pitched tirade at some unfortunate miscreant, a tirade which increased in pitch and intensity as it progressed. The frantic monologue would suddenly cease and after about five seconds of silence, between two and four sharp cracks would ring out as leather impacted on skin. The door would then open and shut once more and the top corridor returned to its former tranquillity.

When we were in Second Year, in April 1967, those of us lucky enough to be drawn out of the hat were chosen to go on a cruise on the Dunera to Amsterdam, Copenhagen and Bergen. This was a tremendous experience and, for many of us, our first trip abroad. It was a fortnight of Clogs and Waterbuses and Little Mermaids and Trolls and the composer Grieg's house at Troldhaugen - and some "probably" conspired to consume Carlsberg. We didn't realise that the Dunera had a murky past since it had been used during the war to take internees to Australia under pretty inhumane conditions. Later groups also went on the Uganda.

Iain and I finished top and fourth in 1A and, in 2A, first and third. I always reckoned that I was hard done by since, on this Academic course, Art alone among the practical subjects was included in the final reckoning and I was hopeless at it, which cost me a lot of marks. I never, ever passed an Art assessment and was glad to be rid of fading washes and poster paints at the end of Second Year, even though Buckie and Gordon Harvey had been marvellous teachers. Tecky also went by the wayside but music remained along with PE as non-certificate subjects. We did, however, change music teachers from Ian Seeley, who relished bashing out tafatiffys with a spoon on people's heads, to the inspirational Ian Bowman.

With the subject of our choice between History and Geography also being dropped – I stuck with History – this left a fair bit more time to tackle our eight "O" Grade subjects in greater depth. Poor old "Hairy Hugh" MacDonald really struggled to impart Chemistry at all, so it was possibly despite rather

178

than because of him that I went on to do a degree in the subject. Sometimes he would lose the rag altogether and his face would turn an alarming purple colour, which was disturbing for a man alleged to have a heart condition.

Our teacher for "O" Grade and Higher French was something of a mixed bag. Head of Modern Languages Ellis Stuart known universally as "Curly" - was a hard man to please and took his subject very seriously indeed. Curly's idea of a treat on the last day of term was to let you read Paris Match magazines – in French. A passionate supporter of General de Gaulle, Curly was in deep mourning when Le General died late in 1970. Curly also demanded very high standards and if you forgot the past historic tense of "savoir" or mispronounced a word whilst reading aloud from Daudet's "Les Vieux" or "L'Agonie de la Semillante", you could pretty well be guaranteed a knuckle on the side of the head. On one occasion, Iain forgot to do his homework and, miraculously, was allowed to bring it the next day, by which time he had copied Curly's own answer off the board. He was given 17 out of 20.

However, I did have a personal reconciliation – a rapprochement - with Curly in later life when he discovered that I had taken to reporting on his sporting passion of shinty. I was summoned to his house in Heathcote Gardens for a discussion on the game and towards the end of his life – around 1994 – I visited him in Ach an Eas Old Folks' Home. Totally unexpectedly, and for the first time ever, he actually unwound and told me of how he had spent the war working for British Intelligence behind enemy lines in France and Poland. I wish he had told me more about this brave service, but for Curly, this was already quite a lot.

By Third Year, one of our favourite after school pastimes, before heading home, had become "going to Frankie Jew's". Now this was the universal nickname of Mr FC MacKay who took over the small grocer's shop at the bottom of Hill Street from Tom Galloway and both Frank and his tiny, packed premises were institutions. The name was fully justified for a man who would charge smokers (I was never one) 3d for a single fag.... and an extra ha'penny for a match. When you bought anything, Frank, who called even the smallest of boys "sir", would instantly state the price and hold out his hand for the money. But when it came to giving you your change, there was always just that brief hesitation before he would part with the cash. Frankie Jew was Ronnie Barker's Mr Arkwright long before his time.

One of our favourites from Frankie's was called Frosty Fingers - frozen ice lolly material in a sealed polythene sachet. You tore the corner off with your teeth and then proceeded to suck out the contents as they melted over the next several minutes. Frankie Jew made an absolute fortune out of school kids, not only from the Academy but also Crown School right across the road, and Millburn.

One Inverness Royal Academy ritual was accessing games periods at the field which was half a mile away on Victoria Drive. Classes would walk from the school, wheeling bikes where applicable, along Crown Circus, down Cawdor Road, briefly into Crown Drive and then a left turn into Victoria Drive itself which, like Balnacraig Road on the other side of town, was still an unmetalled dirt track. That took up a fair chunk of any double period and at the end, if it was Periods 4 and 5, you always worried about

180

getting away again in time to get back to the school for First Sitting at lunches at 1245. In fact, by the time you got down, then got changed and performed the reverse process at the end, there wasn't much of your 80 minutes left for activity.

The spring of 1969 heralded our first exams for the Scottish Certificate of Education Examination Board – the "O" Grades of which we sat eight, Subjects with an Alternative syllabus had pink papers, otherwise it was white. For most of my group of friends it was English, Maths, Arithmetic, Chemistry, Physics, History or Geography, French and Latin. A couple of days before the exams started, Bill Murray, who seemed to get all the odd jobs in addition to being Head of PE, would arrange a squad of prefects to set out the desks in the hall in strict rows and columns.

Then the invigilators, many of them retired teachers, took over. The Chief Invigilator was Bill McKell, a retired Director of Education with the Colonial Service in Nigeria. The son of the legendary Drumnadrochit schoolmaster AC McKell, Bill was the first boy winner of the Howden Medal in 1922 – a year when he also managed accidentally to hit another boy on the head with a shot whilst practising for the school sports. The boy made a full recovery. For some reason or another, that year's Latin paper was quite easy and I finished it in 50 minutes and indeed for anyone hoping to get a good grade at Higher, "O" Grades, brought in as part of a major reform in 1961, weren't especially challenging.

Inverness Royal Academy offered a formidable variety of extra-curricular activities ranging from drama to Scripture Union and from debating to the Outdoor Club. Much of my extra-curricular interest was in sport but there was also the Country Club which was a Young Farmers' Club run within the school by Patsy Forbes who came from farming stock near Nairn. Most of the members had no agricultural connection at all, which proved to be my undoing at the Young Farmers' quiz when slides of various "beasts" flashed up on a screen for identification. Haplessly, my best response was "A cow?" and when asked what kind it was, I could only upgrade my answer to "A brown cow?".

The Country Club offered a wide range of activities like farm visits, walks, dairy visits and a highly thought of speechmaking contest where Iain, Richard and I won the national final in the Muirtown Motel early in 1970. Our coach was the recently retired Head of English Jacob "Fritz" Mowat, the nickname being a result of an Orcadian accent so incredibly strong that he was taken for being German – and indeed the urban myth when he arrived in the school in 1944 was that he was one of Hitler's secret agents.

Patsy was so delighted with our success that she took Fritz and his three 16 year old proteges in their school blazers through to the bar afterwards and had the trophy filled with cider. Fritz's guttural response was unforgettable - "Butt! Das ist alkoholische!" The cider in question as only mildly "alkoholische" but we made up for that in the Loch Ness Hotel that evening.

Richard and I were among the fortunate half dozen appointed as prefects at the start of Fifth Year, the other boys being Pete Grant, Stewart Donald, Dave Barnett and Ali Cameron, younger brother of the future "Mr Loch Ness" Willie Cameron. In Sixth Year, Pete and Stewart went on to become Captain and Vice Captain with Jane Bullock and Norma Spiers their female counterparts. For the first time in 1969, new prefects had silver rather than gold braid put on their blazers to distinguish them from holders of sports colours.

Becoming a prefect meant quite a lot of responsibility such as attending school functions and, in the case of the girls, making the tea at events like parents' evenings and the school sports. Fourth Year girls, making a pitch for prefect status the following session, used to embrace tea making with vigour, running the risk of being branded "sooks". Prefects also had a fair bit of disciplinary input with official powers to hand out detentions for latecoming and lines or a 500 word essay for small misdemeanours.

The Smokers' Union at the Midmills Road corner of the building had very good lines of sight, enabling members to stub out their cigarettes before any raid by officialdom got within 20 yards. This problem was once solved in unique fashion when a squad of prefects piled into Malcolm Ferguson's car which stopped out on the street and the whole lot were nabbed before they knew what was happening.

As in all schools, smoking was pretty prevalent and while it is something I have always abhorred, plenty of my friends did indulge. Frankie Jew made a great deal of money out of this habit among both Royal Academy and Millburn pupils which does raise a question. How many lives may subsequently have been lost to a habit which began within that very environment? One school Christmas concert even featured a special version of the 12 Days Of Christmas where each verse ended with "And a single out of Frankie Jew's".

Smoking and drinking were commonplace at

school dances, especially the Fifth and Sixth Year ones which were great social occasions. At the end of November, normal PE stopped and was replaced by "Danseen" where a record player in a smelly gym provided the wherewithal for practising Velitas, Gay Gordons, Eightsome Reels and the horrendously complicated Pride Of Erin. Bill Murray and Miss Buchan, later Mrs Seeley who was followed by Sheila Macdonell, combined forces for what wasn't an altogether popular activity and it also created a particular dilemma. When invited to take your partners, and in the sobriety of the gym, what did you do? Allow self consciousness to force you to edge across the gym at a snail's pace..... or risk being thought distinctly uncool by sprinting over to grab the pick of the bunch?

Extra-curricular performing arts operated on an industrial scale at Inverness Royal Academy with drama, opera and a large choir and orchestra all healthily coexisting. There were easily enough resources to produce a major opera and play more or less simultaneously, and in 1969-70 Ian Bowman did Mozart's Cosi fan Tutti while Shakespeare's Macbeth, produced by Jimmy Girvan, also played to full houses – and they were very often full and overflowing. Peter McConnell's Macbeth dismissing Brian Howlett as a "cream faced loon" and Harry Nicoll's "Oh! By whom?" response of Donalbain to the news that "thy royal father's murdered" are unforgettable. In earlier years dramatic offerings such as The School For Scandal and The Browning version had proved equally popular as did a wonderful production in 1966 of Carmen starring Ranald Smith and Shona Kinnon.

Harry and Janis Kelly, who both went on to

become professional singers, played big parts in Cosi while the following year, Janis was a magnificent female lead in Purcell's Dido and Aeneas.

The school choir was around 100 strong, albeit some of them motivated by the cynical end of missing RI on Tuesday and Thursday mornings in order to attend choir practice. I was a member of the choir, which also did superb Christmas concerts at Craig Dunain Hospital. However, my limited ability to read music meant that while I was happy to sing along with Handel's Messiah and Haydn's Nelson Mass, the latter performed both in Ness Bank Church and Fort Augustus Abbey with a combined choir from the two schools, I had to admit to Ian Bowman that Mozart's Requiem was just too far outwith my comfort zone.

Some of the titles reveal that a lot of these works were quite high brow, but when it came to the school orchestra Fred Short, who was also the woodwind instructor, took a slightly different approach. As an ex-Army bandmaster, making arrangements was food and drink for Fred and we received great accolades at the Inverness Music Festival for performances of his versions, specially crafted to the resources he had available, of everything from Dr Zhivago to The Scaffold's Lily The Pink and a Hoedown. More conventionally, he also arranged the opening movement of Beethoven's First Symphony where a lack of bassoonists was made up for by less skilful clarinettists like myself honking out that line on our lower registers. We had a number of accomplished performers and at one school concert, cellist Margaret Crean brought the house down with her rendition of Saint Saens' The Swan.

Fifth Year, however, had to be mainly about

Highers, although my extra-curricular activities continued alongside the study of six subjects, and the major distraction of captaining the school team on the Television Top of the Form quiz. Of the eight "O" Grade subjects, Arithmetic automatically disappeared along with the controversial treatment of Latin. With the possible exception of parts of Curly's Higher French, I have to say that I greatly enjoyed all six subjects, especially since they were overwhelmingly well taught. Mind you, assimilating topics as diverse as the Unification of Italy, Integral Calculus, Macbeth's Act V soliloquy, Millikan's oil drop experiment, Daudet's short stories and amphoteric oxides was a considerable challenge.

My prelims all went well, especially Chemistry which set me on the road to my eventual degree subject, but that was the one that possibly suffered most from the pressures of Top of the Form. I did get my six A passes, but not quite as comfortably as I might have wanted in my chosen subject of Chemistry. In all, four of us got straight As – Iain, Peter Grant, Barbara McBeath and myself - and two more got 5As and a B.

This meant that, from the whole of Inverness and much of Inverness shire, six pupils got A passes in five subjects. Nowadays it's perfectly possible - good but possible - for a single local comprehensive, of which Inverness has five, to have six pupils in S5 with five A passes. However, this is not the forum to examine possible reasons for this dramatic hike in the award of top grades over the period of half a century, much of which I witnessed at first hand in the classroom.

For many of us, this made Sixth Year something of a skive since we already had what we needed for unconditional acceptances through UCCA for the universities of our choice. Initially, I made a rather too ambitious course choice of Sixth Year Studies in English, Chemistry and two of the three Maths papers. I also did only the Physics theory out of interest although I was known to observe that there was no point in doing the practical anyway since Physics experiments never work!

A couple of weeks in, I decided that the Maths papers were too much like hard work, so I dropped them both and took on a couple of periods of music and loads of PE. Now, the music was a brilliant opportunity to sit in Room 24, the small music studio, and listen to stuff in the company of not one but two teachers. Ian Bowman and Ruth Grant made it a staff-pupil ratio of two to one and I picked up just so much. The several periods marked PE on my timetable amounted to a rather more cynical dodge. Sure, for a few of them I would go out running and gave the impression that this what I did with them all. But, in the absence of an actual class, this was also an excuse to travel the country in Iain's family Hillman Imp or to wander along to Morrison's for a pie.

Iain had a March birthday so passed his test early and had liberal access to the red Imp. The usual four of us would contribute 10d each and the resulting 3/4d purchased half a gallon of petrol – easily enough for a jolly to Nairn or Beauly for coffee or, strangely, Abriachan. Skiving off down town was also commonplace and on one occasion, Iain and Richard were nabbed by Jimmy Johnstone the Depute Rector. However they managed to persuade him that they had been at the Post Office looking for decimal currency leaflets – even though it was a public holiday and the PO was shut. Decimalisation, with its New Pence and half-penny coins, came and went largely without incident.

There were still classes to be attended and we did Anthony and Cleopatra and Death of a Salesman in English while Chemistry produced a moment at which I didn't turn a hair at the time, but can now lose sleep over. My project was on distilling solid coal to produce coal tar and I decided (why I now cannot imagine!) that I needed to do a practice distillation with two liquids that mixed. Once I started supervising these projects myself as a teacher, I would have told the pupil straight that such a distillation with a naked flame was neither safe nor necessary. Then I would also have screamed in sheer terror at the suggested distillation mixture – carbon disulphide and benzene! - about 200ml of it. So much for Health and Safety!

At the time, benzene was in the process of being declared carcinogenic and if that lot had ignited in the naked flame there would have been the most almighty explosion and massive amounts of poisonous, choking sulphur dioxide would have been produced. But my teacher not only approved the experiment, he sat there marking jotters while a potential fatal catastrophe was unfolding. This total recklessness and near tragedy still bothers me half a century on.

In the spring of 1971 a few of us sat the Edinburgh University Bursary competition where I did five English papers, two Chemistry and, improbably, one in Geography which I took up again with someone to one tutoring from Jimmy Johnstone. And by happy coincidence, the venue for this last exam of my secondary education was precisely where I had sat the last one in primary school. Promotion and Bursary were both undergone in the extremely comforting surroundings of the General Purposes Room in Dalneigh School. Pete Grant and I took the top two places in the General Subjects section which was miserably endowed since Pete got a pittance and I got no cash at all - just the kudos.... and credit for my contribution to a half holiday for the whole school.

That year, for the first time, pupils were allowed to leave school immediately after their exams. Previously you had to stay to the end of term to qualify but I was happy enough to remain anyway. It was an enjoyable few weeks with no classes to attend but plenty to do such as run the publicity and box office for the double opera production of Dido and Aeneas and Richard Rodney Bennett's All The King's Men. The latter was performed by the junior school with the Little Drummer Boy played by Callum MacKintosh - before his voice broke and he returned to the school as a hefty rugby forward to teach PE and Guidance.

After my final prize giving in the Playhouse, just months before it burned down, I emerged into the sunshine and took a final walk up Stephen's Brae, back to the school to collect my maroon duffel bag from the prefects' room. I then departed the place – as a pupil at any rate – through the same boys' door as I had first entered the building six fulfilling years previously.

CHAPTER 9 – TOP OF THE FORM.

Soon after my Fifth Year in school began in August 1969, the Rector stood up at assembly and made an announcement that would change my life quite radically. Inverness Royal Academy had been chosen by the BBC as one of 16 schools to contest the 1970 series of their hugely popular Television Top Of The Form quiz. The programme, hosted by Geoffrey Wheeler and with its distinctive march signature tune, drew audiences of millions. The radio version had begun in 1948 and was extended to TV in 1962, running until 1975. An all-girls Academy team had contested the radio quiz in 1962 but had been eliminated in the second round.

The school was asked to produce a short list of about a dozen candidates from S5 and 6 to be interviewed by the programme's production staff who would choose a team of four. The first round tie in this knockout would be recorded late in January 1970. Eddie Hutcheon had been appointed team manager and would be in charge of identifying the dozen pupils before proceeding to oversee whichever quartet the BBC chose.

It didn't take long for Eddie to swing into action and all interested pupils were summoned to the hall to tackle quite a long list of written questions. From that test, the contenders were partially narrowed down and further tests, including the use of a buzzer system created by the Physics department, eventually identified the twelve. The buzzer apparatus was very important because Top Of The Form didn't just involve general knowledge; a large proportion of the questions were offered to the first person to buzz in, and reaction time was crucial.

With some relief, I made it through to the BBC interview on a Friday afternoon in December as part of a group which came mainly from the Sixth Year. It was preceded that morning by an important Chemistry test and the coincidence of much of this Top Of The Form experience with studying for and sitting six Highers would loom large in the coming months.

The interviews were conducted by Bill Wright, the series producer, and his PA Mary Craig who was a real Woman Friday. Originally from Glasgow, Mary was a brilliant organiser and problem solver, playing an important role alongside her boss in the running of that programme - and then on Mastermind which Bill went on to conceive and found in 1972.

We were interrogated in small groups but apart from the questions they asked, it was clear that they also wanted to gauge our personalities. Yes, they were very much in the market for finding bright kids but they were producing a TV programme, so the participants all had to look and sound the part as well. Afterwards, there was the feeling that one particularly clever member of S6 failed to get in because of an unfortunate manner and an uncomfortably high voice.

I certainly felt I had held my own with the questions and I received a definite murmur of approval when I reeled off the D Day beaches in west to east order as Utah, Omaha, Gold, Juno and Sword. To me, this was bread and butter, since my dad had landed on Sword Beach on D Day + 2 and over the years I had spent hours sitting in smoke filled rooms listening to 51st Highland Division veterans reliving their experiences.

At 4pm I went to the school library and had

barely sat down when Irene Anderson, a Senior Prefect, burst in. She announced that Bill and Mary had gone off to get their train, but before they left they had revealed that I was definitely selected along with Margaret MacDonald from Sixth Year. They would announce the other two on Monday.

That certainly made my weekend and also my parents', whilst additionally sparing me the suspense of the expected long wait. On the Monday, as promised, the school received a telephone call to say that the other two would be Andrew MacDonald and Irene. This left me as the baby of the team since I was the only representative of Fifth Year, although my classmate Iain Innes was named as a reserve. Iain and Andrew both went on to gain law degrees but, tragically, both died close to the age of 60.

It was at this stage that team members were asked to fill in a very detailed questionnaire about their school subjects and personal interests and Mary Craig was completely up front about this. Audiences, she told us, wanted to hear contestants getting questions, and quite difficult ones, right. These questionnaires therefore helped the question setter, Boswell Taylor, to make the questions themselves difficult but answerable while also differentiating between teams.

To be honest, this also made contestants appear just a bit smarter than they really were. We may have been answering quite erudite questions, but these were drawn from areas of personal interest and academic study. So while, for instance, I must have seemed pretty smart answering a question about the role of Count Cavour in the Unification of Italy, this was from a specialist area of study in Higher History.

The first round, away to Falkirk High School, was scheduled to be recorded on Friday, January 30th. I have always wondered if the school had a modest say in that since our Higher prelims finished the previous day. My three team mates had already encountered their main diet of Highers the previous year so for them Top Of The Form ran alongside lighter academic demands in Sixth Year, while I had to contend with the whole lot together.

Although there was no payment involved, the BBC did look after us very well. Instead of travelling to Falkirk on a bus with the 40 supporters the school sent to cheer us on, the team and Eddie went down on the early morning train and returned by sleeper. Given the state of the A9 at the time, this seemed a welcome blessing. After being taxied to the school, we were greeted by our opposite numbers and given lunch and a tour of the place. Then it was into the lions' den of an assembly hall packed with home fans who could easily out-cheer our travelling support of 40.

Our order of battle, left to right as seen by the audience, was Irene, Andrew, Margaret and myself. We just didn't know what to expect of the Falkirk team but, whilst remaining firmly realistic, it occurred to me early on in Eddie's many practice sessions that I seemed pretty quick on buzzer questions. Each programme opened with eight of these and they also made up the final round to add to the suspense and excitement. The recording itself was preceded by a rehearsal of identical structure and I reckoned that if we could win this, preferably led by an early buzzer blitzkrieg, we would gain a big psychological advantage.

And so it transpired. I really got torn into them

for all I was worth in the rehearsal's opening round, from which we emerged with a lead of something like 10 points to 4. We went on to win that rehearsal quite comfortably, also hitting hard in the final buzzer round, so progressed to the real thing with our tails up. That then unfolded very much as before and we ran out winners by 51 points to 34 to our delight, Eddie's and that of our travelling support.

After the recording there was a long wait for the sleeper so we went to the pictures. We strictly shouldn't have been there because the film, Easy Rider starring Peter Fonda and Dennis Hopper as two drug crazed American bikers, was an X certificate. However Eddie must have been happy enough for us to see it. Easy Rider was preceded by a black and white comedy "short" about the building of a council toilet. It starred Roy Kinnear and became memorable only in its final scene. The day's acute tension was finally released when we all burst into spontaneous hysterics at the schoolboy humour of the toilet being unveiled - revealing a plaque announcing that it had been built through "Pubic Subscription".

Then it was off to the station to catch the sleeper home, waking up to a cup of tea on our way over the Slochd before arriving in the cold, grey Invernessian dawn. We soon found out that our return by train had not perhaps been an entirely good idea after all since our supporters, on our behalf but in our absence, had had the mother of all parties on the bus home. But I didn't have to wait long since on the Saturday night a few pints of under age, celebratory lager and lime were then drunk with Stan, Iain and Richard in the Loch Ness Hotel.

The next milestone was transmission of the tie, which was not until the evening of Friday 13th March and at that time it was still in black and white. The BBC had asked us to reveal the result to as few people as possible to retain an element of anticipation, but with 40 supporters also in the know, it was difficult to keep a lid on this. On the other hand, in between, a lot of people came up to me and said they hoped Friday 13th wouldn't be unlucky for us, so the public in general must still have been in the dark. In the decades to come, I would discover quite a widespread belief that more broadcasting is live than is really the case.

Around this time, I was also captain of a team from my Boys' Brigade company which had reached the UK finals of that organisation's quiz in Cardiff. This was on Saturday 14th and there was just time after watching the transmission at home to jump into a waiting car and get to the station to catch the London sleeper. We missed winning that contest by a single point on a trip which briefly delayed what became the frequent and often embarrassing experience of being stopped in the street and congratulated on my TV performances.

There was then a hiatus of around six weeks before recording our quarter final at home to Leominster Grammar School from Herefordshire. This was on Tuesday April 28th - right in the middle of my Highers. The BBC arrived mob handed several days in advance and started to lay masses of thick cables through the corridors linking their microphones and cameras in the hall to their Outside Broadcast vans in the car park.

With study leave now started, I had some time on my hands and perhaps made the mistake of sitting in the hall watching the engineers instal their equipment and build the set on which we would sit on the Tuesday afternoon. This definitely increased nerves which were already on red alert due to an acute awareness of the expectation heaped upon me after my performance in the previous round.

The Leominster team duly arrived and we entertained them in the girls' prefects room. There they presented us with a glazed pottery miniature of a Herefordshire Cow, which for decades to come enjoyed pride of place in various Rectors' offices. From the prefects' room it was only a short walk to the hall where we, as the home team, were greeted by rapturous applause when we came in and took our places. Captains had not been needed in round one, but for some reason were required this time and the BBC assumed that these would the second team members along. However Eddie insisted that I should be our captain and I wasn't sure whether to be grateful for his confidence in me or to bemoan the extra pressure this brought.

This quarter final produced our worst team performance of the whole Top of The Form experience and also my own poorest individual one. I no longer have a record of the score but, having narrowly lost the rehearsal, we had to come from behind in a low scoring contest and belatedly squeezed home by something like 36 points to 29. It was a close run thing but we had made it and my athletics training diary records that in the evening I still had enough energy left to complete a session of 6 x 300 metre runs at the Harriers at Fraser Park. But our Top Of The Form dream really did quite nearly die that afternoon.

It was thick and fast after that. Just two weeks later, with my Highers still not quite finished, we had our semi-final, also at home, against Lymm Grammar

School from Cheshire. This was a real crunch encounter for two reasons. Firstly, the winners would go through to the final so would be guaranteed a place in that summer's Trans World Top Team contest against Dutch schools, involving a three week recording tour of the UK and the Netherlands. But secondly, that Lymm team had looked worryingly impressive in their first round tie although their quarter final hadn't yet been broadcast.

Although our blitzkreig tactic conceived at Falkirk hadn't really worked against Leominster, we just stuck with it on a day where a large company of gods must have been looking benevolently upon me. After the first buzzer round in the rehearsal Geoffrey Wheeler, in that less formal setting announced, to great hilarity from the home support - "And the score is Lymm 2, Charles Bannerman 14". We won that rehearsal pretty convincingly, once again creating the psychological upper hand.

In the competition itself, my buzzer finger was almost as active and, going into the final quickfire section 33-26 ahead, we sailed home by 59 to 31. This means we must have answered 13 questions in that final run in. It was an outcome which prompted celebrations not only in the hall but also on the top deck of the dais where we were just thrilled at the prospect of another competition and an all expenses paid three week working holiday.

This show aired on Friday June 5th and the Scottish press must have been at something of a loose end after the national football team failed to qualify for the World Cup in Brazil, where England were defending their title. The Daily Record must therefore have invested some of that spare capacity for hyperbole in its report of our win which asserted that: "Most teams have one super brain. Inverness's star was Chas. Bannerman whose solo performance was dazzling."

If truth be told, I had by then acquired something of a reputation as the team's top scorer, especially on these quick fire questions, which created a rather unfortunate misunderstanding. In a casual conversation in school, I had attempted to describe the very high levels of concentration required by saying: "I get the feeling there's just me, Geoffrey Wheeler and the buzzer." However someone misinterpreted this as a claim to be somehow monopolising the quiz, and this was the implication when these words were used to caption a school magazine photo of me in action.

I must still have been on a high after that broadcast and it boosted my running. Despite torrential rain on the grass track at the Bught, I set a 400 metre best at the Inter School Sports the day after and broke that again with a record at the North Schools Championships a week later before winning the school track title. Between Top Of The Form, athletics and sitting six Highers, these were among the most productive weeks of my life. It was unrelenting.

At least the Highers were over by the time of the final in Salisbury against the combined forces of two boys from Bishop Wordsworth School and team mates from the South Wilts Grammar School for Girls, where the final would be recorded. Things had begun to overlap by now and the final was actually recorded on May 21st, a fortnight before the semi was televised. This trip away also brought with it the relief of being able to dodge the clarinet solo I'd been entered for at that week's Inverness Music Festival, an ordeal I dreaded far more than any TV recording.

We set off from Dalcross Airport the previous morning with Eddie as chaperone. Having checked in at the BEA desk in the wooden hut which passed for a terminal, we boarded what was probably a Vickers Viscount for the first hop.

At Abbotsinch, as Glasgow Airport was still called, we transferred to what was my first ever flight in a jet, and on the descent, Eddie got severe earache from the pressure change. Heathrow seemed from another world and so did the massive, chauffeur driven limousine that carried us to our final destination the King's Arms, a traditional Old English hotel right outside Salisbury Cathedral. On arrival, Eddie even allowed us to have a half pint of bitter - the first time I had tasted English beer, which I discovered was rather good!

I found Salisbury Cathedral fascinating and spent much of the following morning exploring it with Andrew. However this visit almost made us miss the final! We discovered a spiral staircase leading to the tower and up we went for a look. But when we descended, we found to our horror that someone had locked the ancient, stout wooden door at the bottom of the stairs and here we were trapped in a tiny landing. All we could do, whilst trying not to panic or yield to claustrophobia, was to shout loudly and hammer on the door. Mercifully, an elderly cleric soon appeared to let us out, declaring in a broad Wiltshire twang: "Oi thought oi 'eard someone hollerin' there!"

It was a roasting hot day and when we got to the South Wilts Grammar School, most of the pupils seemed to be sunbathing on the grass. We were introduced to our rivals, including their captain Tom Owen who, from what we had already seen, was clearly going to be a formidable opponent. He also seemed to latch on to me and, shortly after introductions had been made, grabbed me by the arm and led me away for a private chat. It may just have been a friendly gesture or there may have been an element of attempted gamesmanship, but we got on extremely well and continued to do so during the summer tour. Meanwhile we also had to present our hosts with the porcelain model of a Highland Cow which the Rector, borrowing the idea from Leominster, had sent Louise Munro, then the junior school secretary, down town to seek out.

Television sets can be extremely warm places when powerful lighting has to be deployed and on such a hot a day and having to wear blazers, the climate on that stage was almost unbearable. It was a huge effort for all eight of us to think straight but both teams performed well. Having lost the rehearsal, we then went down 61-51 in the final itself, with Tom reproducing all the form which made him the best opponent I came across during either series. So no Wise Owl trophy for us, but we bade our opponents farewell with the desire expressed on both sides to meet again that July in a contest involving Dutch opponents from Eindhoven, Deventer and The Hague.

The final was transmitted on Saturday June 20th and, despite our defeat, was well received locally. A five week break followed before the start of the Dutch epic on July 25th. It was pretty well a case of opening my Higher results and flying straight off again to London but with two differences. Eddie wasn't involved this time and the other three had now left school while I contemplated starting Sixth Year the following month.

We were booked into a posh Bayswater hotel, the Leinster Towers where I quickly settled down in front of the TV in my room to watch Iain Stewart and Ian McCafferty take 5000m gold and silver for Scotland at the Commonwealth Games in Edinburgh. The third quiz British team was Aberdeen Academy who had been judged the better semi final losers – possibly due to the heaviness of our defeat of Lymm Grammar. The Aberdeen team included my fellow athlete James Treasurer. Inspired by the Commonwealth heroics, we then wet for a run in Hyde Park and were quite thrilled to meet a group of athletes already on their way home from Edinburgh.

Andrew's first gesture of largesse at the hotel was to offer to buy me a pint of lager. That flamboyance was somewhat deflated when it emerged that these cost 5/6d each, compared with 3/3d in the Loch Ness and 2/4d in the Lochgorm at home. On the other hand, this was almost the only alcohol that had to be paid for since everything was free at that evening's introductory party for teams and production staff at BBC Television Centre at Shepherd's Bush.

This followed a fascinating tour of the building, including watching a recording of Dixon Of Dock Green, before I fell foul of inexperience on my first exposure to unlimited free booze, much of it cider. I was copiously sick afterwards in the sink in my room and felt absolutely dreadful on the following morning's London bus tour, which I couldn't wait to end so I could collapse on to my bed.

Our next stop was Shakespeare country and a stay in what our tour guide patronisingly insisted on telling the Dutch was "Strat - ford - up - on -ay - von". This included attending The Two Gentlemen Of

Verona at the Royal Shakespeare Theatre before heading back south to Salisbury for recordings. We weren't involved yet but were able to cheer on our Salisbury and Aberdeen compatriots.

From London, we flew to Edinburgh... or rather, after an aborted attempt there, we made an extremely hairy alternative landing at Glasgow in bad weather, and a late night bus trip. Edinburgh was simply a weekend tourist stop and it was by bus that on the Sunday night we went up the still tortuous A9 to Inverness, where we had two matches to play. Our hotel was the Kingsmills, which wasn't quite as luxurious as it is now, but in view of the next day's contests, I opted instead for a decent sleep at home.

These matches, on Monday 3rd August, were against Eindhoven and Deventer before meeting The Hague in the Netherlands, and the school hall was taken over for a third time by a vast array of OB equipment. This time the audience was a bit different, with fewer pupils due to the school holidays but the recordings were opened up to the general public, including our parents.

I have lost any record of the score in a fairly narrow win over Eindhoven but our relatively comfortable margin against Deventer was 42-30. Helped greatly by a home crowd, these back to back victories very much put us in the driving seat in the overall contest. However it must be said that the Dutch were competing here in a foreign language which must have made the buzzer questions in particular quite challenging. Throughout the entire experience, I just could not get over the quality of the English spoken not only by our opponents but by large numbers of ordinary Dutch people.

With the Transworld Top Team "Owl" trophy - Hilversum, July 1970.
Margaret MacDonald, Irene Anderson, myself, Andrew MacDonald

That evening we attended a Civic Reception in the Town Hall. Inverness was our final port of call in the UK and from Dalcross we flew, via Glasgow and Heathrow, to Amsterdam's airport at Schiphol. Our base in the Netherlands was a very up market motel just outside the city which did excellent "Broodje mit ham of kaas" (bread with ham or cheese) for breakfast and we were liberally entertained throughout. Although we could not be paid for our efforts, the BBC more than compensated by giving us 30 shillings a day in "expenses", which grossed me twice as much in a week as the previous summer's job in the filling station.

We actually spent very little of this apart from the odd Wimpy in the UK while in the Netherlands it was souvenirs and the odd glass of Heineken. Hospitality there, provided by host broadcaster NCRV, was every bit as good as the BBC's, with one novelty being a number of traditional Indonesian meals. The Dutch East Indies have colonial links similar to ours with the former British Empire and it was here that we had our first experience of Genever – juniper flavoured Dutch gin.

Our NCRV hosts were producer Dick van den Ende and his PA Ellie Klootwijk while presenter Kick Stockhuysen also made occasional appearances. Much of the time we did the Dutch equivalents of the "Frae Bonnie Scotland" cliche, involving cheeses, clogs, Delft china and natives wearing not kilts but traditional black and white suits. Oh yes, and an Amsterdam tour which included the Red Light District, but in a waterbus.

Recordings were in the Dutch broadcasting centre at Hilversum, so a dozen years on I could at last say I had been at one of the names on that old radio with its thermionic vales. We used a full studio theatre and Provost Bill Smith's wife Lily even travelled out to support us.

We needed to win or draw our last match against The Hague to take the series but lost 33-27 and I did have one grievance at a "refereeing decision". Asked what "The 100 days" were, I buzzed in with what I thought was the quite concise answer - "The period between Napoleon's escape from Elba and the Battle of Waterloo in 1815" - but it was knocked back for some obscure reason. It didn't cost us the match, but it did rattle me a bit.

This defeat left both The Hague and ourselves with two wins out of three at the top. The series was therefore decided by a tie breaker based on the teams' percentage of correct answers across their three matches. This took several agonising minutes to work out so the recording was stopped. It was then restarted with the announcement that, by a very narrow margin, Inverness Royal Academy were the Transworld Top Team champions of 1970. The Owl Trophy was duly handed over and urgent phone calls were made to Inverness.

It wasn't quite finished, though. There was also an International match the next day between UK and Dutch select teams and I was fortunate enough to be included alongside Tom Owen, Morag Ogilvie the Aberdeen Academy captain, and one of the Salisbury girls.

Here I was quite amused to see members of the Dutch audience brandishing a large floor brush - a clear reference to Dutch Admiral Maarten van Tromp who, in the early 1650s, used to tie a broom to his masthead as a symbol of having swept his enemies from the seas. What they seemed not to realise was that, half a century before the Act Of Union, the war in question was solely against the English while here, half their opponents would be Scots.

This final programme provided me with what I have always regarded as my finest individual moment on Top Of The Form. Throughout the series, a number of buzzer questions involved identifying classical music, which was one of my special interests, and this always provided us with valuable points. This time, they gave us the final bars of the Mendelssohn Violin Concerto and the first couple of seconds happened to include a very distinctive high note on the solo instrument which enabled me to crash in instantly. I was quite overwhelmed to hear the production team's spontaneous off-mic gasp when I gave a very quick correct answer. I still cannot listen to this movement, and in particular that tell tale violin note, without thinking of that TV studio at Hilversum.

In the end, Team GB prevailed by a comfortable margin and the broom bearers beat their retreat. Then we all prepared to leave for home in high spirits, with my own higher than most after contributing to the double.

Our four programmes didn't go out until late in the year which meant that for most of 1970, I found myself very much in the limelight and frequently stopped in the street for congratulations which sometimes got quite embarrassing. I am even now still occasionally reminded of these campaigns long gone, but for some reason all this public exposure never seemed to count against me on under age drinking expeditions.

This Top Of The Form experience was life changing because I emerged from it with much higher levels of self confidence and with a different perspective on a lot of things. Having appeared in front of audiences of millions, gone were my crippling inhibitions about speaking in public. I also acquired a great regard for the BBC which carried forward to over 40 years of freelance broadcasting for that institution. These early experiences indeed probably spared me much stage fright in various situations in later years. And for decades until I retired in 2013, I would walk past the school trophy cabinet in the Culduthel Building, spot the Owl sitting there and remember this great experience with fondness and pride.

Two years after our place in the sun, Bill Wright went on to conceive and produce Mastermind, based on his experience of wartime interrogation by the Gestapo. His involvement prompted me to apply for the second series in 1973 and, having turned 20 just before the recording I believe that, nearly 50 years on, I am still among the programme's youngest competitors.

So for me, the implications of the Rector's 1969 announcement that the school had been invited to take part in Top Of The Form had been very far reaching indeed.

CHAPTER 10 – SPORT.

As a career, it was a desperately slow to start, as accounts of my complete ineptitude during my Dalneigh School days have already shown. However sport quite suddenly became a major part of my life and would very much remain so. As an athlete, I never really got much past "respectable" but as a coach I aspired to some quite advanced international levels across several decades.

During that same period, I developed a second career in sports journalism, both written and broadcast, initially also in athletics, then ultimately reporting on shinty and football for national media. But during my childhood days, Inverness really wasn't much further along the sporting road than I was myself.

In the 1960s and for some time after, the place was something of a sporting desert. There was plenty relatively local, low level activity but the Highlands barely made a mark on the national and international scenes. This was perhaps unsurprising. Facilities were very few and far between, external communications, especially by road, were extremely poor and public consciousness of sport was much more limited.

That deficit also created something of an irony. Although these barriers to sporting achievement were steadily overcome and success grew, obesity also began to flourish. General fitness levels started plummeting, not only in Inverness but across Western civilisation. Lifestyles changed dramatically and our two solid hours of football behind St Valery Avenue or staying in the swimming pool until Donnie Ross inspected our fingertips, would steadily go out of fashion. This conspired with other factors, including increasing affluence, to promote a more sedentary lifestyle and the retreat of the fitness culture – ironically alongside an eventual growth in sporting opportunities and achievement.

So what did Inverness have to offer sports people in the 1960s? The jewel in the crown was the swimming pool but there wouldn't be a running track until the 1980s or a sports centre before the 90s. The Queens Park cinder track was opened with great pomp in the late 50s but was hardly used and soon fell into disuse and disrepair when its management committee went defunct. There were the pitches at the Bught but not a great deal else for amateur football which still never failed to flourish. At that time and right through to the present day, the Bught has been graced by iconic amateur and welfare outfits such as Painters, Gellions and Bankers. Meanwhile judo and badminton clubs struggled on in various halls and there were several bowling greens such as Bishops Road, Craig Dunain and Planefield Road.

And then there was the Town Council's policy not to hire out any of its sporting facilities on a Sunday. Sabbatarianism was still hanging on stubbornly and it was well into the 1970s before initially limited Sunday lets became possible.

Football clubs had proliferated since the 1880s. Inverness had four Highland League outfits until the 1930s before Citadel departed the fray, leaving the town to those intense rivals Thistle, Clach and Caley. They were pretty successful at Highland League level and even grabbed occasional morsels of Scottish Cup glory. They would also have been willing enough to brave the tortuous A9 and compete in the Scottish

Football League. However that particular prejudiced protection racket conspired to exclude everything north and west of the Aberdeen - Perth diagonal until the mid-1990s. Indeed it was in the 1960s that Clydebank chairman Jack Steedman proclaimed that Highland clubs would get into the SFL "over my dead body".

My regular visits to Telford Street didn't survive for long after I left Dalneigh School. The sudden and unexpected changes to our circle of friends when we went our separate ways from primary school were also reflected in my pastimes. My new social circle at the Royal Academy weren't football fans to the same extent and the Academy's rugby culture also took over fairly quickly.

Another factor was that, not being a good player, the remaining incentive to stick with football - subscribing to the norms of my peer group - had also gone. The game had less of a hold on me and I quickly lost interest in it. I did continue to follow various clubs' fortunes but it wasn't until the emergence of another incentive nearly 20 years later - the opportunity to report on the game for the BBC - that my interest was rekindled.

The big local football event of the mid 60s featured not an Inverness team but Ross County who played Rangers in Dingwall in the second round of the Scottish Cup in February 1966. It had been a frosty winter and eventually, to get the game on, County well had to ruin their pitch to make it soft enough to play on. Rangers won 2-0 in front of a packed afternoon midweek crowd said to be 8000 strong - including many from Inverness. Indeed it was said that many strokes of the belt were administered in Inverness schools that week for truancy.

There were no national rugby leagues until the 70s and while clubs in the central belt found friendly fixtures easy to access, it wasn't quite so easy for Highland RFC. Another decade on, though, Highland would be among the first to fly the Inverness flag regularly in major national competition by reaching Scotland's new top division in three consecutive bounds.

For several years Highland, who would not have a youth development structure for some time, used to play on the Queens Park infield with a 1st XV which included two well known local worthies.

At this time, Colin Baillie was a young and enthusiastic PE teacher at both Millburn and the Royal Academy and was not yet the major figure in the development and coaching of sport in Inverness that he later became. Colin had lost an eye in a childhood accident but the resulting disappearance of stereoscopic vision didn't prevent him from becoming a fine rugby full back who could kill a Garry Owen at a stroke. Colin, who survived being strafed by the Luftwaffe in his native Dundee, was born the day after Churchill made his "Never in the field of human conflict...." speech. I have yet to decide whether it was the RAF or the birth of Colin Baillie that finally deterred Hitler from invading!

Then there was Marshall Grant, formerly Marshall Notman, who had been a fine young middle distance runner but had now become Highland's hooker. Marshall did continue his running activities on his morning roll delivery round. He would leave his driverless mini van rolling up the street in second gear while he ran to and fro depositing bags of rolls on front steps.

Shinty, especially before it introduced national leagues, was another pretty localised activity. In the north competitions, Inverness at least had opponents such as Beauly, Lovat and Glenurquhart within half an hour of their traditional base at the Bught Stadium. Here was a significant facility, even though the stand was already struggling to cope with the years, and the shinty club guarded it jealously. This wasn't without justification since shinty had done a lot to put it there and it is now a sub-national facility for the game.

Clachnacuddin Cycling Club still toured the highways and byways and were often to be seen competing at various Highland Games where Ivor Reid was king of the grass tracks. For curlers and skaters, Inverness Ice Rink appeared in 1967. From 1961 to 1969, the town had no athletics club since Inverness Harriers, having fallen on hard times, went into abeyance and existed in name only.

So much of that Inverness sporting scene was extremely localised, and for any of the Highland League teams, a journey on the A96 (then arguably the best road out of town!) to Peterhead or Fraserburgh would have seemed like to the end of the earth.

This is a far cry indeed from a Scottish Cup winning football team which once finished fourth in the Premiership, a resident three times world curling champion in Ewan MacDonald, a rugby club which is now rising up the national hierarchy for a second time, an athletics club which has had a remarkable production line of internationalists, two shinty clubs, Lovat and Glenurquhart, within 15 miles of each other with recent national trophy successes and a lot more. A great deal has changed for sport in

Inverness since the mid-1960s.

At Dalneigh School, I was poor to the extent of embarrassment. Last to be picked for kickabouts, permanently consigned to the handwork class rather than be inflicted on football or athletics practice, last in the school sports and with only minor redeeming features in non-running activities like swimming and cycling. It really seemed a lost cause and, with basketball at PE added to the list of abject failures, it started looking like more of the same at the Academy.

It's difficult to pinpoint where the change began, but let's try the 1966 school sports heats where, in the school's system of physical ages, I was placed in the smallest category, Group T. To my absolute shock, and the astonishment of my parents, and wearing a World Cup Willie T-shirt, I won my heat of the 250 yards and finished a modest seventh in the final - but from little acorns. Into Second Year I won the 2AB cross country race which replaced class rugby in frosty weather. Twice round the school field, twice round Millburn hill and twice round the field again was the route. From there, my interest already primed by the Tokyo Olympics, I became drawn to competitive athletics and was much encouraged by Walter Banks, a family friend who was also a senior official. This progressed through more school sports, including the senior track title in 1970 and 71, and representing the school at a number of championships. It was an attachment which would last a lifetime.

My only explanation is that, at around 13, I underwent an early growth spurt which converted dysfunctional limbs into quite efficient and stronger ones, although my woeful eye for a ball would never

Winning the 350 yard race at
the Royal Academy sports, June 1968.

improve. That could be mitigated far better in rugby than any other ball game and I found myself playing at wing forward for the Second Year XV, before moving on to scrum half and then wing three quarter.

My first home game was in Second Year against Rannoch School and my dad came to watch. However he saw precious little thanks to two trips to Raigmore Hospital, first with Iain Steven whose collar bone was broken when Brian MacIlwraith practised a tackle on him during the warm up. My dad got back during the game but had to retrace his steps with Stuart Donald and his dislocated shoulder. MacIlwraith, by the way, seems to have had a talent for crunching bones and became a well known local osteopath!

Soon after, we went to play Gordonstoun's preparatory school at Aberlour which was a complete hoot and a total eye opener. We could barely play for laughing at a culture and way of life none of us had ever imagined before. It started with the captains as we left the bus when Their Chap, a genuine Tim Nice But Dim, loudly greeted Our Chap (Peter Grant), telling him how AWFULLY pleased they were to see us and would we care to step this way? I have often wondered if what we were looking at here was an unconscious caricature of his own chinless wonder father. The rest of us tailed in after them, wetting ourselves.

During the game itself, which we lost, the touch line was jam packed with little Hooray Henrys emitting a constant, near hysterical chant of "Come ON Abbalaaaah!! Come ON Abbalaaaah!!" Inevitably "Come ON Abbalaaaah!!" was imitated ad nauseam on the bus on our way home from this first insight into how the other 1% live. And the High School thought WE were posh!

I also got a selection for North of Scotland Schools under 15s in 1968 but my rugby career

215

really went on the back burner from Fourth Year. My limited ball skills eventually found me out and I also wanted to concentrate on running.

Rugby matches between the blue shirted Academy and Millburn in their black strips had a great local derby feel on a playing field the two schools shared. It was also a field which caused great pain within both institutions after Dodo Sinclair of Millburn cut his leg and became seriously ill with tetanus, leading to mass vaccinations for both pupil populations. Long since forgiven, I've felt ever since an empathy with Dodo over that – an empathy enhanced by his father "Butch" having been the "young lad" among my grandfather's railway colleagues.

In 1969 I punctured my finger with a spike whilst long jumping at the field (I still retain the sensation of metal impacting on bone) and needed a booster of some sort. I had to run the 800 metres at the Inter School Sports two days later with an extremely sore backside!

Because I just missed the 31st July cut off to remain an under 15 in Fourth Year, I was projected straight into senior rugby. I played relatively little, and always for the 2nd XV, but this was different since Millburn was still a junior secondary and our games were often against Gordonstoun and The Abbey School in Fort Augustus. The Royal Academy really wasn't in the same league as Gordonstoun and our 1st and 2nd XVs played their 2nds and 4ths. Gordonstoun pupils had the reputation of staying on for quite a long time until they got a qualification; the guy I played opposite on the wing looked absolutely ancient and was going slightly grey. We dubbed him "grandad".

Games against The Abbey were closer and a lot more sociable than the stand offishness at "Colditz In Kilts", which was in between having Princes Charles (who dubbed it as such) and Andrew in it ranks. Little did we think that there was such horrific abuse going on against some of the Abbey lads we played against since this only emerged decades later. As a young teacher I once accompanied a colleague to the Abbey with a school team and we two staff were lavishly entertained with beer by monks who appeared to be the epitome of geniality.

Inverness Royal Academy played a huge part in my early sporting development but extending this outwith and beyond the school was entirely on my own initiative. Bill Murray, the Head of PE, put a great amount of time into coaching rugby and athletics (he had an intense dislike of football) but showed no interest at all in his pupils joining cubs in the community. I actually felt quite awkward when my interest in athletics prompted me to join Inverness Harriers after the club was re-constituted in 1969. The concern was what Bill might think, and it took more than a year for me to wear a Harriers rather than a school vest at the Highland Games.

Bill thoroughly disliked change of any kind and was an out and out elitist. With echoes of Miss Jean Brodie, he had not "My Girls" but "My Boys" - an "in group", of which I was a member and which steadily evolved as pupils came and went from the school. I also see Bill's dislike of non-school clubs in parallel with Miss Brodie's antipathy towards the Girl Guides, which she saw as competition for her own influence over "Her Girls". Movement from Inverness Royal Academy to post-school sport was extremely sparse - for instance FP's of Inverness's "rugby school" were conspicuous by their absence from Highland's great team of the mid 70s. This would change radically under different management in the school's comprehensive era at Culduthel.

It was amid this distinct lack of enthusiasm from Inverness's leading secondary school that Inverness Harriers made its 1969 comeback after eight years in abeyance. However, the other two secondaries played a major part, with Miss Horne from the High School and Colin Baillie, who by now was full time at Millburn as Head of PE, both very much involved. Indeed, Colin quickly became Chief Coach at a time when the only place the club could get to train was Fraser Park. This led to not a few disagreements with Highland Cricket Club who had used the park for many years

There were no field event facilities whatsoever and the "track" amounted to a 300 metre circuit with tight bends. There was also a bit of a hill outside the pavilion and when Baillie got us to run 400s, he always made sure we had to go up that hill twice. It seriously understates Colin to call him a hard task master and we were convinced that, alongside the flurry of abrupt peeps on his whistle and barked instructions, his underlying training philosophy was "If it's not making you sick, it's not doing you any good." One cold night I got cramp in both calves, and it fell to Colin and Brian Milne to pull the knots out. And Colin did just as effective a job, despite Brian's professional experience of pulling. He was a gynaecologist!

Many of the seniors, such as Dave Fotheringham, Ronnie Ross and "Mr Inverness Harriers" Ian Tasker had been members during the club's previous incarnation. Due to the lack of field and throwing facilities, we didn't see much of the "heavies" like Ronnie and Tony Cohen, also a well known shinty player, who had to look after themselves.

We had a group of juniors which included Calum MacDonald and Pat MacKay from Millburn and Gordon Melville from the High School. Academy pupils were like hen's teeth. Willie Junor had been there from the start in March 1969 but it wasn't until late June that I decided to brave Bill Murray's displeasure and go along myself. I decided that I was dead keen on the sport and I wasn't prepared to allow school disapproval to deprive me of this new opportunity.

This was a club which was then unrecognisable compared with the production line for Great Britain and Scotland internationalists that it became into the 1980s and beyond. The competitive diet was primitive, amounting to little more than Highland Games in a short, two month summer season where we would compete for prizes to the value of something like 30 shillings, or a little more. My mother's cupboards soon became full of toast racks, bedside lamps and sets of teaspoons.

The early star turns were four female sprinters. Ann Leith was another Academy pupil while Diane Roodhouse, Josephine Gunn and my old Dalneigh friend and desk tidier Audrey Grant were all High School girls. All four were capable of national standard performances under the coaching of Diane's dad Ted, but opportunities were as difficult to find as they were for those in other sports which were based at the wrong end of the A9.

Harriers training also had its lighter moments and by 1970 I had my moped. This meant that Audrey and Anne were among the illicit passengers who got a "seater" for the 600 yard trip down to

Frankie Jew's at Kingsmills for post-training refreshments.

There was also a second Harriers summer (the club only met from April until August) at Fraser Park before the Town Council eventually relented in 1971 and let us have the Bught. Additional sessions could also be obtained there by climbing over the gate when there was no groundsman around.

This change of facility attracted a bigger group of young kids, including Kevin MacDonald whose future lay firmly with football. From Caley he moved on to Leicester and then to Liverpool where he won the 1986 English League and Cup double. One year before that double triumph, he was in the Hysel Stadium in Brussels to meet Juventus in the European Cup Final. Thirty nine people were killed in a tragic crowd crush which had a massive effect on English football.

Athletics competition continued as a purely local tour round the Highland Games, where the pipe band was quite capable of entering the field just as athletes went to their marks. There was also the odd local meeting like the 1969 Avoch Gala Sports where the handicapping was done on the spot, based on how big you were and whether you came from Inverness. I dubbed this Inverness Harriers' first overseas trip since we all travelled across on the Kessock Ferry. Unfortunately, the perpetually late Ian Tasker had to take the next boat since his black MG shot along Kessock Avenue just as the Rosehaugh's ramp was being raised.

In the 800m, three of us battled shoulder to shoulder to a point of exhaustion in the finishing straight, only for ex-Inverness Provost Bobo MacKay to emerge from a knot of officials and declare: "Och you'll have to do another lap lads. We're not quite ready."

At the end of the period covered by this book, April 1972, I was on the point of returning to Edinburgh University for my first summer term there and my debut for the University club. This would provide an eye opening insight into far more orthodox athletic competition which was light years away from what would persist in the North for almost another decade. But that comparison also highlights how rudimentary and localised sport still was in Inverness for more than three decades after the war. After that, the sporting environment would undergo a welcome and wide ranging revolution and much credit for blazing that trail must go to Nairn MacEwen and Highland Rugby Club whose pioneering rise up the national leagues in the mid-70s was an inspiration to all.

CHAPTER 11 – TEENAGE FREEDOMS.

There is one partial gap in my moving picture of a decade and a half's upbringing in Inverness and it corresponds to the first 12 months after leaving Dalneigh School. Memories of my earliest days at Inverness Royal Academy which coincided with this period are crystal clear but not of activities outwith school.

This is almost certainly because of the social vacuum created on changing schools. That saw longstanding friendships from Dalneigh Primary drift apart alarmingly quickly while new ones took some time to develop. One moment I was in a Primary 7 class with many other kids who were also my leisure companions. And then, bar Iain who was also with me in 1A at the Academy, they had all disappeared into a different class or a different school.

This drifting apart is something I was just vaguely aware of at the time and its full significance only became apparent much later. But these first months at the Academy were something of a social desert until I steadily built up a new set of friends. It was quite strange, however, that no longer being educated within the same classroom could have such a rapid effect on friendships of so many years' standing. It's also interesting to speculate as to whether this might have happened to the same extent with the availability of modern communications technology?

One way our new group of friends got to know each other was during trips down town, often on Saturday afternoons. The mid 60s were still the heyday of adolescents going to cafes and, at 13, we wanted to break our way into what the older ones did. The Cafe George in Queensgate was a particular favourite and so was Morrisons above their baker's shop in the market. Before long, glasses of coke had extended to Saturday lunches and Morrisons' pie and beans were to be savoured.

Alternative sources of nourishment could be found in Woolies. It was around this time that they introduced Pick 'n' Mix which had a standard charge for a quarter pound and you used a little trowel to shovel your choices into a white paper bag. This was then weighed by the assistant – but usually ended up heavier, and more expensive, than you had expected. By this time they had white top pan balances rather than the seesaw efforts with brass weights of previous generations.

However, the real bargain in Woolies was a bag of broken biscuits. Rather than throw damaged stock away, they would keep these in a special container and you could fill a bag for just a penny. Too many broken biscuits were probably the main reason for the rare occasions when I would go home and not eat all of my tea.

One other attraction was The Record Rendezvous which began life on the north side of Bridge Street, close to the Gellions, before it moved in the late 60s to Church Street. Browses in both premises were extensive at a time when you could still get a 7 inch single for 6/8d while a 12 inch LP (Long Playing record) like Sergeant Pepper cost 30s.

Then there were EPs (Extended Play) which were still 7 inches, but the grooves were more densely packed, giving perhaps a couple of singles per side. The great thing about record shops was that they would let you listen to your prospective purchase in a booth before you made up your mind.

Although they have been making a comeback, these records - latterly known as vinyls to distinguish them from the many intervening formats - are now dated technology. I remember as far back as 1993 listening incredulously to a Currys salesman telling me that I would be far better buying a CD player since records would very soon be obsolete. What I dismissed as sales talk became reality very quickly – and CDs are now obsolete.

The technology behind the "record player" is actually very simple and doesn't even require electricity. If you use the vibrations of whatever you are recording to create bumps in spiral grooves on a master disc you can then use that master to make many copies. If you then place a needle – which originally was just that before the sophistication of a diamond or sapphire stylus – in the groove and turn the record, then the bumps make that needle vibrate and you retrieve the sound. Early "gramophones", as still shown on the HMV logo, used a trumpet arrangement to amplify the sound but this was later upgraded to electronic amplification into loudspeakers.

The earliest records rotated at 78 rpm – hence their title "78s" - and this meant they didn't last long even though they were 10 or 12 inches in diameter. By the early 60s these were well on their way out but record players could still operate at 78 rpm to play them. Otherwise, it was 45 rpm for singles and EPs and 33 for LPs which had been ground breaking technology in the 1950s. It was always great fun to play a record at the wrong speed and have a great laugh at how bizarre it sounded – like the Chipmunks if you upped a 45 to 78.

There's something about early autumn evenings that fascinates kids in their early teens. Whenever the nights draw in, youngsters – possibly seduced by the novelty of returning darkness - begin to take to the streets, usually just to "hang around". We were no different, but now the motivation had changed to something more legitimate and peaceful than throwing penny bangers up garden paths.

The vast changes I underwent from the age of 13 were much wider reaching than the physical growth which sent me into a belated career in sport. Apart from my voice breaking – fortunately without collateral squeaking and growling - there were other hormonal and psychological changes. These included a growing interest in girls and an accompanying concern for one's appearance.

The latter wasn't helped by a period of facial acne, although that could have been a lot worse and much more drawn out. Even so, I found this quite traumatic and spent a lot of time anxiously examining the effects using my parents' dressing table. It was one of these old-fashioned models with a front mirror but also rotating leaves left and right which gave a proper view as well as a fascinating illusion of depth created by infinite reflections. This unsightly source of much adolescent angst was finally eliminated by a course of oxytetracycline antibiotics from Dr Farquharson.

These advancing hormones also stimulated the growth of facial hair, and it was probably at some point in 1967 that the need to shave emerged. Well, perhaps not quite the need, but the accumulation of enough down on my cheeks to justify the use of my father's razor as a novelty and something to boast about. Shaving foam wasn't universal by this stage so I used the more conventional shaving soap applied by a brush. I rather disliked the sensation of that brush but this was overcome by the sense of achievement. As a further status symbol, I adopted quite lengthy sideburns and indeed stuck with them for some years.

It was into the autumn of 1966 that we began to hang around with this group of girls who had been in my class at Dalneigh and were now in other classes at the Academy. Everything was transacted on bikes and I was the proud owner of a brand new blue Raleigh Riviera which even had three gears operated by a very trendy twist grip. Unfortunately, it didn't retain its pristine condition for long after being consigned daily to the bicycle graveyard along the Academy's Midmills Road wall.

At this point I gained another friend, Robin Clark who had gone to the High School but had an interest in one of the female members of this group. This led to an association which lasted for several months, punctuated by an unholy water fight transacted not only in Robin's garden in St Mungo Road but also from windows on both storeys of his house. Robin got into serious trouble when his parents found out. Eventually the difficulty of sustaining a friendship between two secondary schools intervened and we drifted apart.

One thing we did together was a novelty to both of us – clothes shopping. Hitherto, my mother had bought everything and I had shown no interest at all. But, with adolescence beckoning and girls to impress, that changed and I became very picky about what I wore. Johnstone's in the Market was one of the "go to" outfitters in this era of elongated shirt collars, often with buttons, and crimplene ties with square ends. My pride and joy was a white shirt with a button down collar and lots of reflective gold coloured vertical strands down it, topped off with a black crimplene tie with a red and white striped band at the top, along with a pair of tight brown trousers. The sheer excitement of the novelty of these clothes purchases leaves an abidingly happy memory.

This was also a period of change at the barber's shop. So far, Diggar had simply run the clippers right across the back of my head and had been pretty ruthless with the top as well while I simply listened to his patter. But now, here I was instructing him to remove a lot less before topping the whole job off with lashings of Brylcreem. Indeed Brylcreem, a white oily emulsion with a trademark aroma, much loved by the Teddy Boys of the previous decade, became so *de rigeur* that I kept my own supply at home as well.

All of this set me up perfectly for a truly fascinating social novelty – the Young and Old dances which took place usually at the Lochardil Hall or the Midmills Scout Hall. Once again we were allowed to go to and from these unsupervised on a Saturday night but on one occasion coming home from Lochardil we got lost and I panicked and rang someone's doorbell, asking directions to "get back to Inverness". We were only in Green Drive!

These were our entertainments a year or so before the novelty of the disco hit Inverness and we attended these dances much of the way through secondary school until they eventually went out of fashion. Music for Velitas, Miltiary Two Steps, St Bernard's Waltzes and Gay Gordons was provided by a band comprising five or six men who were mainly doctors. Certainly my own GP Willie Ross, who had also been my dad's wartime comrade, was one of them and another was Monty Hadley who had kids just above me in school. These were memorable, highly civilised evenings where people of all ages got together in a manner which was by now in its dying days.

We also used to gather in each other's houses of an evening and these gatherings were one factor which contributed to my dad buying a record player early in 1967. If kids were going to gather they needed to listen to music. As with other non-essential items, my parents had been just slightly behind the curve. The main reason they didn't get a record player too early was that they wanted to hang on in the hope that I would abandon my liking for the pop music of that golden era of the mid 60s, or at least acquire an additional taste for something they considered more acceptable.

And as it happened, alongside the house gatherings, a somewhat latent interest in classical music came to the forefront. This had been around since late primary school and its upsurge was part of wholesale personal changes, some of which I have already described. Possibly the first manifestation was finding myself spending a lot of time in Bruce Miller's in the market or the Record Rendezvous reading up about classical music from the backs of record sleeves. I also bought myself a copy of Teach Yourself Music, one of a hugely popular series of little books with black and yellow dust jackets on all manner of subjects from Physics to Football – both of which I also had.

At this point, my only access to classical records was at the home of our family friend, my former

Lifeboy leader George MacKintosh in Leys Drive. George not only had a top of the range Grundig player but also very many high quality Deutsche Grammophon LPs. While my parents and George chatted (quietly), I would listen – enthralled - to Beethoven, Bach, Schubert and other composers less well known. Buxtehude, anyone?

Classical music almost became a fixation and my enthusiasm was such that they eventually relented and bought a record player so our early lack of one meant that I never bought any pop records. Oh... apart from one Seekers LP. As with other items, it wasn't a bottom of the range job either. There were still very few stereo players about in 1967, but my dad parted with £36 to Mason's at the bottom of Crown Road for one.

Unfortunately, there was some fundamental fault with the thing and after several trips back to Mason's for repairs, a refund was eventually arranged. I don't think my dad really trusted stereos after that, so it was replaced by a good quality Decca mono player – but not before I had acquired a number of stereo records which now just produced mono sound.

After that, a procession of budget classical albums came into the house, and especially Music For Pleasure discs which could be acquired amazingly cheaply for 12/6d each. Among my earliest acquisitions were Handel's Water Music and a Vaughan Williams selection including The Wasps overture, while George gave me one or two of his old records including Bach organ works and Beethoven's Emperor Concerto.

Around the same time, I attended my first concert outwith a school trip. I paid 7/6d for a front balcony seat to hear Alexander Gibson conduct the

Scottish National Orchestra in the Playhouse and was completely blown away by the excitement of live instruments delivering the first frantic bars of Dvorak's Carnival Overture. As that fixation grew, I could often be found, pre Eden Court, at concerts in the Playhouse or Inverness Musical Society chamber recitals in The Arts Centre in Farraline Park, and I became progressively less interested in pop.

In the summer of 1970, there was a pop concert at Telford Street Park but I was nowhere to be seen. Our very different musical tastes did indeed create a very minor disconnect between me and the rest of my friends. It was hence for two reasons that I would later feel somewhat underwhelmed sitting in smoke filled halls of residence rooms listening to Deep Purple.

My musical preferences also meant that I didn't feel all that comfortable during my relatively few visits to The Scene discotheque when it opened in Haugh Road in 1968.This had nothing to do with the moral outrage that briefly swept through Inverness's more conservative classes at the thought of the utter degeneracy of youngsters dancing to recorded pop music for the first time in the town's history. The Caley Hotel had been one thing, as long as its renowned dances to the likes of Harry Shore's band stopped before midnight on a Saturday.

To Inverness society's more conservative members, these were tolerable – as generally were the special late licences through which local clubs could get money from hotels for sponsoring them on their behalf. Similarly, crowds of Inverness youngsters went on buses to "The Strath", the legendary dances in the Strathpeffer Pavilion which were said to attract up to 1000. Indeed, that is the number it's claimed attended The Strath on Saturday 4th January 1963 when The Melotones were playing. This left just 19 four miles away in Dingwall attending a concert by a still relatively obscure quartet of Liverpudlians known as The Beatles.

During the 60s, when dancing to live bands was very popular, there were famous local groups such as The Flock. But for some reason the idea of dancing in a dark room to records introduced by a probably long haired "DJ" was initially too much for some of the older generation to stomach. The Scene did get the go ahead though, and I did attend, albeit not all that enthusiastically since I have always felt quite self-conscious "dancing" in a certain way to music with which I cannot identify.

All of our visits were to the unique late afternoon openings which The Scene had for younger school kids and this felt very strange indeed. Still in our school uniforms, we would rush through the Crown and down Godsman's Brae to bop around in the dark behind thick black blinds to the likes of The Mighty Quinn, or Silence Is Golden before the strange sensation of emerging on to Haugh Road in brilliant sunshine. The Scene didn't survive for long but what it did do was to create the precedent of disco dancing in Inverness and this quickly took on. It was at The Scene that the seeds of Dillingers and Mr G's were first sown.

Despite my conversion to classical music, I still look back on that second half of the 1960s as a golden era for pop. Perhaps this is partly due to the personal awakening that was going on, but I also believe that the songs of that brief period were very special. The Summer of Love took place in 1967 and Scott McKenzie's San Francisco epitomised that watershed for the Hippy movement. Other classics from that very special year included Procul Harum's Whiter Shade Of Pale, the Bee Gees' Massachusetts and the Beatles classic All You Need Is Love. Before and after that one, the Fab Four produced Yellow Submarine and Hey Jude.

Then there were more off-beat creations such as Scaffold's Lily The Pink and I Was Kaiser Bill's Batman, a one hit wonder from Whistling Jack Smith. This period was also Engelbert's zenith with classics including Release Me, There Goes My Everything and The Last Waltz. But as the 60s passed into the 70s, my interest in pop music very quickly died. I am just grateful that it had not quite died during such a creative period.

Some of our time was just spent wandering aimlessly round town in between these visits to cafes and record shops. The place was full of exotic retail outlets where Hepworths, Burtons and "John Collier, John Collier The Window To Watch" led the men's outfitters. Saxone, Easiephit and DE (short for The Dundee Equitable) kept us well shod and if you'd spilt coffee on a garment you needed to wear later in the day, then 60 Minute Cleaners were there to help. Two food retailers migrated to the newly erected jungle – Liptons to Lower Bridge Street and, later on, Low's to where Queen Mary's House had been. Then there was that wonderful coffee aroma in Coopers.

There was also the fascination – especially after colour began but wasn't yet in many homes – of stopping outside various TV shops and looking at the vast array of screens. Differences in picture quality were often striking. On Saturday afternoons, especially if there was a big event on, David Coleman's Grandstand and Dickie Davies' World of

Sport were especially popular.

Inverness has a rich history of worthies although this is a trait which has tended to die out in more recent times. Before our era there was Forty Pockets, a tramp like figure who used to hang about and generally entertain the local populace. Later on there would be Suzie MacKay, remembered by many for her habit of chasing passers by and poking them with her umbrella. Born in Edinburgh, Suzie was brought up in a children's home before being boarded out to Farr during World War 1. At the age of 70 she wrote her autobiography A Discarded Brat, a title which epitomises her early life. As late as 1989, when she was 80, she walked the Inverness 10K to great acclaim.

But the two who were most memorable to our group of friends were Granville and Willie Bell. Granville Paterson was notorious for everything from throwing himself in front of cars to his appearances in court charged with... let's just call it offences against fauna, specifically the ovine species. Willie Bell, meanwhile, was a rabid Scottish Nationalist, so rabid indeed that it was said that he had been thrown out of the SNP for being too extreme.

In response, Willie (or Uilleam as he used to style himself in Gaelic) set up his own political party dedicated to Scottish independence by whatever means and on one occasion in the mid-70s he ended up in court charged with some kind of attempt to blow up pylons carrying Scottish electricity to England. In 1974, Willie even stood for Parliament – with Granville as his election agent and a flat in Greig Street as their election office! Needless to say, he failed to unseat Russell Johnston.

Willie's Anglophobia also extended to his

frequent exhortations to English tourists to go home as he tramped the Inverness streets in his kilt and jacket, and it was here that our paths would cross. If we were wandering round town and spotted Willie, we knew that he would be seriously wound up if we let out a big "hoooch!" as we passed him – so inevitably we did just that. However, on one occasion, in the market arcade, I misjudged my subsequent dash round the nearest corner and got caught up in a crowd of people. Unable to make my escape, I received Willie's leather brogue right up the backside.

One thing we never did was go to youth clubs. There was the Queens Own Cameron Highlanders Memorial Boys' Club – often just called The Boys' Club – in Planefield Road which had a formidable record in a number of sports. Then there was The Doc's Club at the top of the Raining Stairs which also attracted a large clientele, but neither appealed to any of us.

So OK... there have perhaps been some hints of geekery in recent pages, so let's even that up with a little of the Hard Stuff.

One major rite of passage of the mid teenage years is, of course, under age drinking and during the late 1960s in Inverness it was incredibly easy for quite young children to get their hands on alcoholic carry outs. I'm sure there were many other similar places across town but our local off licences were Alexander Fraser's and Stuart Walker's which were across Tomnahurich Street from each other. I can barely believe this now, but I may even have still been in Third Year when I went into Fraser's and requested a bottle of cider - only to be asked not my age but "Which kind would you like, son. Woodpecker or Strongbow?"

But at that stage in life, illicit alcohol still played a very small part in our group's lives and this would remain so until around 16. And even then, one thing our group never did was to buy a carryout and go and drink it on a building site or whatever, just for the sake of it. Gratuitous outdoors under age drinking never played a part. It was either a visit to the pub or a carryout before some kind of function.

At home I had been allowed a Babycham or a very small sherry on the basis that a moderate introduction might curb excesses in later life and in general, that approach did turn out to work. What we used to do instead at around 14 was to get cans of innocuous Hunts "lager and lime" or "ginger beer shandy" which had less than 2% alcohol and could legally be sold to anyone at all. These became the bevvy for these parties in each other's houses where we would drink the stuff – reinforced by chocolate liqueurs at Christmas – and then role play being drunk.

The next stage after the Babycham or a tiny sherry when my parents' friends came round to the house was definitely the 51st Highland Division reunion in Perth in October 1967 to mark the 25th anniversary of the Battle of El Alamein. After Monty had done his stuff at the South Inch in the afternoon, the "after party" for our group took place at the Royal George Hotel where many old 5th Seaforths and their families were staying. Now these guys had certainly fought for Britain and my goodness, some of them could drink for Britain as well!

This was probably the first time I realised that the restrained alcohol consumption of my domestic environment was by no means universal and by the time many of them got a few in, their generosity knew no bounds. However my parents managed to restrict what I was given to a couple of small glasses of cider. This didn't even create a little light headedness and the first time I experienced any actual effect from alcohol was at Christmas dinner two months later when I was given a full glass of red wine. However that effect was mild and very transient, and no one offered me the enhancement of a second glass which I would probably have accepted gratefully.

I think our introduction to going to pubs may have been slightly later than some, although totally Apocryphal tales about so and so "getting served" at an unbelievably early age were legion. Many of the fanciful lines shot by some contemporaries would even put Jay from The Inbetweeners to shame. I think it was probably right at the end of 1969, when we were in Fifth Year in school and I was 16 and a half, that we started to patronise licensed premises, initially the Loch Ness Hotel where you could get a pint of lager and lime for 3/3d. Once you had not quite spent ten bob, it was clear that risking another one mightn't be a good idea. The reason I can pin this to late that year is my recollection of the Christmas Carols we sang fortissimo as we walked back down Glenurquhart Road.

At the bottom of the price range was The Lochgorm, one of that roll of honour of famous Eastgate pubs which also included the Albert and The Plough, now long since gone. There may have been sawdust on the floor and it may have been in the same luxury bracket as The Market Bar, but 2/4d was all it cost for that same pint.

Eastgate was also a convenient hop away from

the school and it was in the Lochgorm that we "prepared" for the After Highers Dance in June 1970. The other pre-dance staple was the carryout and it was one such experiment that saw me come to grief for the first time. This would have been December 1969 when we were Fifth Year prefects and hence allowed to attend the Third and Fourth Year dance to keep good order and supervise

Aye, right! I met Richard at the Kenneth Street traffic lights and we duly obtained a litre bottle of Strongbow cider each from Alexander Fraser's. The problem, however, was that we were running a bit late so had to dash behind Serafini's chip shop and deck the stuff in great haste – which was my great undoing. I doubt if our demeanour at the dance was especially prefectorial, but my worst experience was when I got home. For some reason or other, five or six units of fizzy alcoholic beverage were still active and within two minutes of laying my head down, I spontaneously threw up all over my sheets. A typically understanding mother accepted this as a probable deterrent for future indiscretions, and indeed it was.... sort of partly.

The "in places" for under age drinking in Inverness used to change subtly over the years and in the early 1970s the Columba Hotel probably led the field. Across the piece, I have few if any memories of being "asked my age" in any Inverness pub. I also remember coming off the bus from the 1970 North Schools athletics championships and celebrating my 400m record in the Carlton with Richard. Although many under agers went to the then pretty decrepit back bar in the Heathmount, I also recollect indulging in the luxury of brandy and Babycham in the bay wndow at the front when it was part of a small, separate room.

The cosy front bar in the Glenmhor Hotel was another favourite, especially when I came back from Holland with a taste for Heineken of which the Glenmhor was then a rare UK purveyor. It was said that if Royal Academy pupils were there and French teacher Torquil MacLeod came in, there was no cause for alarm or panic because the most likely outcome was that he would buy you a drink.

Torquil was indeed very generous with his drink and when we were still in Fourth Year, in the early hours of 1st January 1969, Stewart Donald and I decided to first foot Torquil who lived on Auldcastle Road with his aged father, a retired Boots pharmacist. It seems remarkable now that two 15 year olds should have been allowed to wander long distances from home in the early hours of New Year's Day. When we arrived at this teacher's house he not only welcomed these two 15 year olds.... but also plied us with copious quantities of gin!

One problem with pubs until licensing laws changed in the mid-70s was that they all closed at 10pm, unless a special late licence could be obtained for a function. Across the land, this led to an unseemly rush to the bar on the shout of "last orders please" at 9:50 and a 20 minute binge until what was often a fairly rigorously applied 10:10pm drinking up deadline. Our group were no less prone to the effects than anyone else and there was the occasion when one of our number had to be helped to his front gate and silently manoeuvred up the path. Silently, that was, until he contrived to kick over the milk bottles, provoking the inevitability of his mother coming to the front door to investigate. The rest of us could have scarpered but we did do the decent thing and waited to make our profound apologies on his behalf.

Another time, one of my fellows decided that he wanted to go round to the house of this girl he fancied and when we got there, he proceeded to lob gravel from the path at the bedroom window. The trouble was that it was the wrong window and we beat a hasty retreat amid a hail of invective from the girl's mother.

On Hogmanay some pubs closed earlier still – perhaps even at 9pm – which left a lengthy hiatus before our next scheduled drink. This would be at midnight at home where we all dispersed before reuniting after The Bells, and we each had our own solution to the delay. Since I came home through Dalneigh School after leaving Iain at the end of Lilac Grove, in the best traditions of Scott of the Antarctic, I used to stash a couple of 250ml bottles of Carlsberg Special behind the fence there for collection on the way back.

Consumed – suitably chilled - at perhaps around 10:30, this was easily enough to keep the pot boiling until midnight since Carlsberg Special is a powerful brew of around 7% ABV. Round about the age of 18, we went through a Carlsberg Special phase but this was really no more than macho showboating because a more vile concoction than what is "probably the most disgusting lager in the world" is difficult to imagine. Some tried to disguise the taste by adding blackcurrant juice but to little avail. It was one of these drinks which you swallowed and then tried to conceal the shudder.

One Christmas Eve in the Tenerife, I was spared the Carlsberg ordeal because after closing time I had to go along to the church to do a reading at the

Watchnight Service, so was able to "downgrade" to vodka and orange without losing face. The Glory of the Lord must have shone round about me that night because I negotiated the text flawlessly while the vodka ensured that I was not Sore Afraid.

Under age drinking, records, fashionable clothes and other luxuries had to be financed and although pocket money rose steadily from the shilling and half crown of primary school days to perhaps ten bob a week or more, this still fell short of requirements. The solution was holiday employment and Iain got a job in the new Caley Hotel and was soon doing a very credible impression of Mr Scott the Head Porter.

I had a fairly generous pocket money supplement from what my aunt and uncle gave me at the end of quite frequent visits and my own first job was in the summer of 1969, in between Fourth and Fifth Year, selling petrol at the Millerton Filling Station. Also working there was Dave Caddell with whom I played rugby and ran in school teams and whose father was a psychiatrist at Craig Dunain.

Hall Thompson was a pleasant enough employer but half a crown an hour was hardly the epitome of generosity. On the other hand, this was supplemented by pretty good tips and if I saw a car come in with an F or a B on the back, I would be sure to speak to the customer in French which often elicited financial benefit – except from Flemish speaking Belgians. There were seldom tips from Americans, though, since they thought our "gas" extremely expensive and would generally growl "fillid up wit regularr"... meaning bogstandard 91 octane.

We had a state of the art petrol pump where a rotating control could deliver 91, 93, 95, 97 and 99 octane, starting at 6/3d for 91 and increasing by a penny per grade. All it did was mix low and high grade streams and if anyone wanted 101 octane – Spitfire fuel in effect – then a separate pump delivered that for 6/8d.

By this time I had developed a strong liking for CS Forester's Hornblower novels, which are almost the only fiction I have ever read post-Blyton because my preference has always been for the factual. While we waited for the next customer to drive in, I would often catch up on a bit of Napoleonic War naval drama.

That job didn't yield much cash but, having just turned 16, there was enough for me to fulfil my part of a deal whereby if I found half the cost of a moped, my parents would pay the rest. A number of boys were getting Honda 50s or occasionally 90s, which were small motorbikes, but my parents weren't prepared to go any more powerful than a moped. This was a bicycle with pedals and marginally more credible than the "mobylette" which was more anaemic still.

So that September I became the proud owner of a Honda PC50 (the PC standing for Pedal Cycle) LST 98H – and an orange crash helmet. It would do about 32mph on the flat and had to be taken up Crown Road to school, which it just about managed without my having to pedal. Its half gallon tank, which it cost just over three shillings to fill, would guarantee more than 50 miles of travel.

The following summer my scope for employment was more limited due to a three week absence touring with the Top Of The Form quiz team. For the first three weeks of the holidays, my dad got me fixed up in the Tax Office at River House where he was Management Inspector, and very pleasant that was too. Apart from filing, one of my main jobs was to check the arithmetic in the tax calculations colleagues had made in this pre-calculator age, before these were sent out, and this was right up my street. My most memorable colleague by far was Lovat Shinty Club legend, the effervescent and extrovert blonde Mary Ann Henton. This began an association, continued through my shinty reporting actvities, which lasted just a few months short of 50 years, only ending when Mary Ann died in 2020.

I turned 17 in July 1970 so my first weeks of learning to drive a car were interrupted by the Top Of The Form adventure. My dad took me out a lot and the more sophisticated stuff was done through the hugely popular Donnie Ross of the Argyll Street based Triumph School Of Motoring. I was never sure if reversing round a corner or the parallel park was the most challenging manoeuvre – probably the former – but by late autumn, I felt ready to sit my test.

It was early December before that took place and when I arrived at the Testing Centre in Ardconnel Street, it was to my horror that I saw the dreaded Mr Cumming walking towards me. This was the man that no learner wanted to see and his reputation went before him. My demise came on emerging from Crown Drive on to Crown Road where I cruised casually in my father's Humber Sceptre out into a stream of traffic to a cry of "Watch out laddie!" from Cumming.

"S**t," I thought. "That's that, then." And so it was. As adolescents do, I returned to school in the vilest of moods, denied forever a place in the prestigious "Passed First Time" club. However I got another chance in January with the much more popular Mr Veitch and duly prevailed. Now I could join the ever expanding group of Sixth Year fellows allowed the status symbol of taking the family car to school, with all the kudos and street cred that entailed.

It was during the summer between school and university, that I visited the dentist for the first time in a couple of years. When we came to Inverness, I attended old Mr MacDonald in Queensgate and if anything ever needed done he would, with a dark suited doctor sitting somewhat ominously in the background, first of all place you in a spartan looking seat surrounded by a matching off-white array from which protruded all manner of drills and other implements of torture. He would then place a smelly black rubber mask over your face, get you to bite on the rubber mouthpiece and switch on the supply of nitrous oxide – or laughing gas because of one of its effects in low concentration – which would send you to sleep.

This, at the age of about 10, was intimidating in the extreme but it wasn't long before you were out cold, although not before experiencing just a few seconds of tantalising unreality as you went under. When you woke up, albeit somewhat disorientated and occasionally feeling sick, it was all over and the worst difficulty was a dribble of blood after an extraction. There was, however, a much easier method of removing loose milk teeth which didn't involve gas or even a visit to the dentist. You would simply tie one end of a piece of strong thread round the tooth and the other end to a door handle before giving the door a good kick and the momentum of the door yanked the tooth out totally painlessly.

However it was pain that drove me away from

the dentist for that couple of years since a new practitioner preferred local anaesthetic by injection into the gum. The thought and sensation of that needle, which he administered with the callousness of an Obersturmfuhrer SS, were just too much for me and I refused to go. By the summer of 1971 intense toothache was making it clear that there was something far wrong. At that time one of the coaches at the Harriers was Eddie Sharpe, a former Royal Academy athlete who had set up practice at the Hilton Centre.

Eddie was full of modern methods, including general anaesthetics by a modest injection in the arm and he took me under his wing. Once again there was that feeling of unreality followed by disorientation but my goodness, this was painless dentistry and I stuck with Eddie's extremely busy and popular practice until he moved to the Channel Islands.

By now, though, Edinburgh was beckoning and with it the next chapter in life – albeit one in which my Inverness ties remained as strong as ever.

CHAPTER 12 - DEVELOPMENTS AND DESECRATIONS.

In the summer of 1945, millions of demobbed servicemen began to return to the UK and with that benevolent invasion there arose an acute housing shortage. Apart from supply, the standard of the housing stock was also pretty low across the country, especially in areas like London, Liverpool and Clydebank which had suffered heavy wartime bombing. Inverness had escaped that trial, although the Luftwaffe had attempted to hit the aluminium works at Foyers. However in terms of housing, the need in the Highland capital was was as great as in most places.

Families found themselves having to survive in the most makeshift accommodation. Initially that could be as dire as army huts and caravans, but before long the "prefab" stepped in to save the day. This was the standard term for "prefabricated home" and what rapidly became distinctive white, cuboidal structures with gently sloping roofs initially arrived on site in prefabricated sections which could be easily fixed together. The huge advantage was that prefabs could be constructed very quickly indeed and colonies of them soon shot up all over the country. In all, the UK provided over 156,000 of these often pre-decorated homes, some of which were made of aluminium from decommissioned military aircraft.

In Inverness, prefabs were no respecters of how posh an area was perceived to be. At one end of the town they materialised in more deprived parts such as Coronation Park and Wyvis Place but there was also a development on Sunnybank Road off Culduthel Road and I believe that some of these, re-clad and thoroughly refurbished, may well still be in use. Many babyboomers retain great pride in having been brought up in a prefab.

And therein lay yet another problem to add to the squalor of a mass of 19th century housing suffering from several years of wartime neglect and ripe for nothing other than demolition. As servicemen came back, something of a population explosion was inevitable; the "babyboomer" era kicked off and lasted into the 60s. This had the knock on effect of further increasing demand for housing and something more durable than prefabs – which turned out to be a lot longer lasting than originally expected – was needed.

Inverness's main response to the need for permanent, high quality housing was focused, albeit not quite exclusively, on two areas – Hilton and Dalneigh. From the late 1940s, new builds proliferated in both these locations at an astonishing rate as thoroughfares such as Dell Road, Temple Crescent, Daviot Drive and Drynie Avenue in what is now "Old" Hilton matched the Saints and the Trees over in Dalneigh.

There do seem to be architectural differences between the two schemes, and indeed Swedish houses are exclusive to Dalneigh, but there are also common features. The respective primary schools, although differently laid out inside, look very similar from the exterior with their white outer walls and large windows. Shops were also provided, and the blocks on Tomatin Road and Laurel Avenue, both with houses on a second floor, could well be twins. Both schemes were also provided with a fine modern church in an era when attendance was still burgeoning.

Another common factor was the sense of community which ironically thrived in spite of the more acute class awareness which still prevailed. As mentioned earlier, Dalneigh – and indeed Hilton as well – accommodated a much more diverse social mix in the post war era than became the case in later decades as the professional classes departed to owner occupied accommodation in Lochardil, Drakies and Holm Mills. Indeed, that sense of community, which transcended a wide social range, certainly far exceeded what would more recently be found in the same streets despite that range now being a lot narrower. On the other hand, the cohesive force of a war, which the entire community had joined together to endure, is long gone.

That sense of community was not of course exclusive to Hilton and Dalneigh which are merely the instances used here. It arched right across society and for every story I have told about life in Dalneigh, readers brought up in this era elsewhere in Inverness, and indeed beyond, will have corresponding memories.

These Hilton and Dalneigh new builds were, of course, all Council houses where you paid your rent and, when repairs and such were needed, the Council provided. You were responsible for your own interior decoration and garden, but much of the rest, including exterior paint work, was undertaken by the local authority.

A city whose population has doubled in little over half a century has inevitably been the subject of continuous house building, so while the post-war developments in Hilton and Dalneigh were turning points, they were also part of that ongoing process. For instance, soon after, flats in Coronation Park and

Wyvis Place and conventional housing in Kilmuir and Benula Roads replaced the prefabs, and filled the gap between Cameron Square and the Ferry. Talking of what has never really been known locally as South Kessock, I have never quite understood how or why anyone could imagine that street names like Bridgeview Drive, Carnarc Crescent and Rosehaugh Road were improvements on Ferry institutions known for decades as North, South and West Drives. It was an unnecessary gesture of Political Correctness before its time.

In the early 60s we made a trip across town to inspect a show house in Laggan Road in the then brand new private scheme of Lochardil, but my parents felt it was a bit too early for them. Not long after, their friends the MacGregors moved into number 1, Balvonie Avenue from which the large Drakies estate spread out. Almost a decade later, as a student lemonade salesman, I found myself amid building sites hundreds of yards away at its far end, trying to come to terms with house numbers in Drumossie Avenue matched in Inverness by little more than the cemetery end of St Valery Avenue. And as Drakies, with its council neighbour Raigmore on the other side of Perth Road, developed in East Inverness, in the West, Scorguie sprang up across the canal from Dalneigh. Then in the early 70s, the construction of "New" Hilton", in part to meet the needs of oil construction, imposed the prefix "Old" on the original scheme.

In more recent decades, the expansion of housing in Inverness has been even more bewildering and has burst right out of the old town boundary, where the increasingly busy Southern Distributor Road has utterly failed to contain the suburban sprawl. I still have no idea where all these people find jobs!

Whilst still on the subject of housing, and just to give a fuller picture, it's worth looking briefly at Inverness's fascinating late Victorian era. It doesn't take long travelling around the place to realise that a substantial slice of its more expensive properties in particular date from the last two decades on the 19th century. Much of the Crown – the likes of Southside, Midmills, Beaufort and Lovat Roads - fall into this category. Alongside this, Crown School dates from 1879 while the old Royal Academy building and the Crown Church appeared in the mid 1890s.

Meanwhile, exactly the same can be said of development in the Big Green area – Kenneth Street, Fairfield Road, Ross Avenue, Rangemore Road and a few others – where the wealthier members of late Victorian Invernessian society also laid down their roots. The 1880s and 1890s provided Inverness with much of its most solid architecture and enduring structures, also including the likes of the Town House.

So, at the time my old stamping ground of Dalneigh and its Hilton counterpart were completed, Inverness appeared to be heading in orderly fashion towards a state of coherent and progressive post-war upgrading. But, as the decade of miniskirts, hippies and the Beatles dawned, no one quite yet had any conception of the architectural catastrophe which was about to unfold.

There can be absolutely no doubt that the most criticised feature of Inverness for some decades now has been the carbuncle buildings which sprang up in its centre, mainly during the later 1960s. This is probably the issue that local residents, and exiles, complain about most and it is absolutely central to the manner in which Inverness was changed in that decade. It all began with the new Ness Bridge in 1961. Its elegant lines possibly lulled Invernessians into a sense of false security with regard to the desecration of the town centre that was to follow. I have never been aware of any coherent account of the process within the Town Council which permitted the architectural upheaval that ensued, although a careful search of Council minutes might well shed some light on it. However, the suspicion has to be that a lot of the decisions were taken in smoke filled rooms in advance of formal adoption by the Council. Perhaps the Highland Club, in plush first floor premises between High Street and Lombard Street but now a rather tatty hostel, played a role. It was said that within its walls much used to be discussed among Inverness's movers and shakers. Inevitably there have been various conspiracy theories and speculation about thick brown envelopes changing hands. Some Inverness folklore alleges that the only way anything as horrific as this could have been agreed to must have involved financial incentive, although no firm evidence has ever emerged publicly.

However I do believe that public revulsion against many of these 1960s aberrations, and especially the epitome of this desecration, Upper Bridge Street, is partly revisionist. I don't remember much adverse comment at the time, but latterly this has mushroomed. Upper Bridge Street has now become a byword for all that is aesthetically repellent in the town but there's a lot more than that. The fact that many of these buildings deteriorated quite quickly has made them look even worse.

There was probably a good case back then for the demolition of at least some of the south side of Bridge Street under the castle. As a vital artery carrying almost all of Inverness's rapidly increasing through traffic, the street certainly needed widening and to this end the Forbes Fountain was removed from the front of the Town House in 1953. Many buildings on Bridge Street were also on their last legs, especially at the back. However, the library and museum opposite the Town House and the unique and picturesque Castle Tolmie beside the river are another matter, although Castle Tolmie may well have affected road width.

The demolition of buildings is one issue, but their replacements are entirely another. I'll admit that to start with I quite liked Upper Bridge Street, simply because it was different. In particular we loved Liptons' Cafe, but I also think there was a novelty factor which soon wore off. More recently, the structure's fundamental ugliness has been greatly enhanced by the Sick Building Syndrome from which so many creations of the 1960s and 1970s now suffer.

For instance Inverness Royal Academy at Culduthel, which opened in 1977, began to deteriorate alarmingly quickly. By the early 2010s it had famously been branded a "slum" by Councillor Dave Henderson, a former pupil of the school's previous premises at Midmills which, dating from 1895, still possess an imposing grandeur. I have always believed that Dave Henderson's highly publicised intervention played a big part in the decision to replace that Culduthel building.

On the north side of Bridge Street, it's easier to make the case for the retention of Queen Mary's House in terms of lost character than on historical grounds. Although Mary Queen of Scots did stay on the site briefly during the Siege of Inverness in 1562, none of the original building was left by the time it was demolished in the late 60s to make way for the aesthetically underwhelming HIDB HQ. All that remained was the original cellar which was incorporated into the HIDB (later HIE) entrance while a Rio Stakis restaurant, now Johnny Foxes, went into the ground floor. The later transition from HIE HQ to flats at least made the outside of this new structure just that little bit less repellent.

The neighbouring Parish Council Offices also disappeared at that time, but the redoubtable Miss Eveline Barron, to her eternal credit, refused to sell the Inverness Courier office, which still survives.

However the former newspaper HQ is but an oasis of normality and visual comfort amid a desert of architectural vandalism. The grand old Caledonian Hotel was also pulverised and replaced by an distinctly unprepossessing cuboidal frivolity which blights the riverside. Its front entrance is on Church Street where Dr Matheson's and Dr Ross's surgery next door also disappeared, but MacLeay's model and electrical goods shop was spared.

The other side of Church Street also suffered. In 1788, a group of local toffs with little else to do after the demise of Jacobitism had inflicted collateral damage on the clan system, met in Inverness. The upshot was the annual Northern Meeting which evolved into a series of late summer events for the upper classes. One of its components was a Highland Games for which the Northern Meeting Park was built in 1864. This is considerably pre-dated by the home of its other big event, the Northern Meeting Ball. As early as 1789 they resolved to build, on Church Street, the Northern Meeting Rooms, principally to accommodate that ball which thereafter was a magnet for upper classes from far and wide. Indeed there is a famous 1954 photograph of Princess Margaret arriving at the event.

By the early 1960s, their Highland Games also having become defunct in 1938, the Northern Meeting was struggling financially. The organisation had tried to make ends meet by letting out the Meeting Rooms to the general public for everything from dances to sales of work and in he case of the former, the place complemented the Caley Hotel across the road.

However, the end was in sight. Eventually they sold the place to a developer, hence opening the door to yet another town centre eyesore. The unsightly cuboid that eventually replaced the grandeur of the Northern Meeting Rooms housed from the start a number of shops, including the new Record Rendezvous. Then there was the ultimate irony. What replaced the palatial premises where lords, ladies, chieftains and princesses had danced the night away beneath grandiose crystal chandeliers was also occupied in part by the DHSS offices... notorious as a forum for down and outs to haggle over their Giros.

And across the top of Bank Lane from the new Caley Hotel, glaring across Church Street at the former Meeting Rooms, is one of the ugliest and sickest looking of all the creations of that 1960s urban desecration. Its interior did valuable service as a Highland Council information point but the outside became a visual affront, although at time of writing, this site is under development – into yet another Inverness city centre hotel.

So within a decade, much of historic Inverness within a 100 yard radius of its iconic 18th century steeple was razed to the ground and replaced by an unsightly concrete jungle. All of this was preceded by the disappearance in the mid-50s of the former tartan warehouse and YMCA building on whose roof sat The Three Graces statue, now beside Ness Bank Church. At least its replacement, initially occupied by A. Cameron and then by McDonalds, is not in the league of many of the other monstrosities.

Other parts of the town would suffer similarly and, to move forward briefly from the timespan that these pages largely cover, the urban decay of the centre of Inverness has continued right up to the present day. And like these architectural indiscretions, some of that decline has also been self-inflicted.

Inverness Castle tries in vain to peer through the architectural sterility of Upper Bridge Street.

The early years of the 21st century have not been an easy time for city centres in general; many have been left struggling by the incessant rise of out of town retail outlets. As a result, all over the country there has evolved a story of large numbers of vacant shops and offices and Inverness has been no exception.

To all of that must be added the manner in which Inverness city centre has become more and more run-down looking, as structures decay and vegetation grows out of neglected roofs and walls. It is easy to be fooled by 20-20 retrospective vision through rose coloured spectacles, but there can be no doubt that Inverness now presents a tatty shadow of the tidy, modest respectability for which the Hub of the Highlands was renowned until a couple of generations ago.

Attempts to rectify this decline have ranged from the carving of absurd and fatuous aphorisms into the city's paving stones to dumping sloping slabs on Church Street with trees growing out of them, and further inanities inscribed. Then there was the drawing at the bottom of Crown Road of the former Inverness worthy Forty Pockets, which had to be rapidly removed when it started falling apart. And all of that before we even consider the series of scaffoldings which have blighted the landscape, propping up burned out buildings. It took years for the jungle of metal poles in Eastgate to be removed after a fire there, and a similar monstrosity on an even greater scale round Viewhill House at the top of Castle Street is showing no signs of departing after more than a decade. There have been valiant efforts by many, ranging from the Inverness Courier to the BID organisation to the Civic Trust but, regrettably, none has been able to stall the downward slide. I have never known the confidence of Invernessians in the fabric of their city to be so low.

And it's not only architectural damage that has been inflicted. I am writing this in the immediate aftermath of Inverness councillors mercifully deciding to remove part of the nonsensical traffic modifications which were an issue of huge local controversy throughout the Covid pandemic. Dubbed "The Lego Brick Road" on account of the huge red and white plastic blocks which demarcated it for so long, the main bone of contention was a one way system round the Castle in order to accommodate cyclists and pedestrians who simply and demonstrably did not exist. There is little to be gained from relating that story in detail, save to observe that some of this self-inflicted nonsense will be retained in other parts of the city, further to blight the local environment and to continue to discourage use of an already moribund city centre.

arguably the sickest building in Inverness across Bank Lane from the former Caley Hotel.

Much of this book has been a celebration of Inverness, and rightly so, but in terms of the physical environment of its centre, it is very difficult to come to any positive conclusion or to indulge in any optimism about the future.

Probably the best I can do is to make an analogy with the iconic wartime photo of St Paul's Cathedral towering intact over the landscape of a blitzed London and translate that 500 miles North to the late Victorian Gothic splendour of Inverness's Town House. With its £4 million restoration completed in 2018, it now similarly gazes out over the legacy of six decades of largely structural vandalism inflicted not by the Luftwaffe but a lot closer to home.

Serene amid the devastation - the refurbished Town House and its grubby neighbour.

CHAPTER 13 - THA LONGWUDGE.

No account of life in Inverness would be complete without a look at one of the city's great binding forces – that uniquely flavoured patois which draws so many of its citizens together. It's a way of speaking which sets Invernessians aside from others, and with only the written word to draw on, this chapter must rely heavily on phonetics, making it the most challenging of all to create.

It must be a myth surpassed in improbability only by the Loch Ness Monster, but it's sometimes said that people in Inverness speak the purest English in the country! The presence of Cromwell's troops in the town in the 1650s has even been cited in support of this theory - even though the locals mainly spoke Gaelic rather than English at the time. The most persuasive case against this myth of linguistic purity can be obtained by standing at a bus stop or in a queue at the bar or when wandering through the Eastgate Centre.

Righ'eenaff, it really is a mightily strange version of Tha Unglash Longwudge that you hear.

I don't think I've ever had an especially strong Inverness accent although this can vary, especially on becoming animated or in the pub or in the company of other Inverness speakers – or especially all three. My every day speech is probably much closer to neutral, although without too much effort I can put on a very convincing "Unvarness ocksent."

Several influences, especially listening to parents, peers and associates, determine how we speak and some seem more susceptible than others. For instance my dad had an English work colleague who, during an earlier posting to Aberdeen, had married a local girl. One day my mum, en route to some engagement, knocked on their door to be told by a somewhat flustered native of the Home Counties: "She's nae gyaan.... she's nae weel!"

Before I went to school, I mainly heard my parents' decidedly Wick enunciations from "up ee rodd", supplemented by similar from Caithness relatives. None of this rubbed off at all. But after going to Dalneigh School, a little of what I heard from my classmates certainly did, although I also believe that some of that was lost on going to the Academy.

One of my richest exposures to Parliamo Inverness was probably standing in the Howden End at the Caley Park on a Saturday afternoon in the 1960s. One of the standards was an indignant "Refaree mun!", usually prefixed by a phrase incorporating a frequently used four letter expletive. Before the game, as the enclosure filled up, you would hear "Howyadooeen Gord" - or "Hame" or "Bri" or "Charl". Inverness Christian names are frequently abbreviated to the first syllable. The reply would frequently be "Achyersee'een it mun. How's yersel?". The phrase "Achyersee'een it" is a classic Inverness invitation to allow one's own observations to judge another individual's status.

In the last days of the Howden End, as tempers about the merger with Thistle became frayed, one of the more polite chants to come out of it was "Yull nevarr kull tha Collee." Back in the day, "Tha Collee" had two meanings because, outwith football, it also referred to the hotel and especially its famous dances. And then, after the game, some fans still like to retire to "Tha Collee Claab" for a drink, failing which "Tha Leejun" or some other "paab".

Many Invernessians take their football very seriously and in a shop one Saturday morning, I overheard one supporter make the anxious observation: "He's go' twooo plurrrsh saspendad an' three plurrrsh unjared." When Sergei Baltacha arrived in 1993 to become manager of Caledonian FC, it immediately became clear that his English was quite poor. One wag from within the club was wryly heard to observe that at Telford Street Park, that could only get worse!

Inverness has, I believe, two very subtly different local accents which are pretty well impossible to differentiate in print. There's what I believe to be the original Invernessian - possibly more evident on the west side of the river where families have lived for generations in Dalneigh or the Big Green or "doon tha Ferree". It's ever so slightly musical in its intonation and selected words can be prefixed by the most subtle and brief "grace notes", almost reminiscent of the pibroch or indeed of the Gaelic language itself.

There are also, of course, these unique and defining Inverness vowel sounds that this variant tends also to share with its sister, a version apparently more prevalent east of the river. This may be because larger numbers of incomers settled in newer easterly suburbs and a subtly different speech then evolved. This one tends not to have the same presence of colour and melody but, while its vowel sounds may be very marginally less marked, they are very much the same ones.

During the war, the Dutch claimed to be able to tell German agents by their inability to pronounce the area of the Hague known as Scheveningen properly. Had Inverness required a similar expression, it might well have been "Byoolee", "Dramnadrochut" or "Clochnaharree". "K'torlatee" even. Equally opaque is that frequent plea in a busy queue: "Stop poosheen an' shuveen!"

Meanwhile "rabburr bampursh" (rubber bumpers) is a gem which highlights where Invernessian speech is placed within the upper respiratory tract. In Aberdeenshire, this frequently originates from somewhere back in the throat, while in Glasgow it's decidedly nasal. But in Inverness the vowels in particular come from somewhere in between these two – possibly just below the pharynx.

What is spoken by Invernessians is more of an accent than a dialect. Accents are variants on the way people pronounce a language's standard words, with differences largely in the vowel sounds. For instance if received pronunciation is "change", a Cockney might talk about "choinge", a broad Glaswegian "cheynge" and a Shetlander would use "chenge". New Zealanders, meanwhile, contrive to make every vowel they can into a "u". In contrast, a dialect tends to have its own unique words such as "quine" in Aberdeenshire, although advocates of Doric may well claim that it is a language on its own.

Inverness seems to have relatively few words unique to the local area, although there are some such as "goolachan", as we used to describe an earwig. This may have Gaelic roots, as does "boorach" - a confused mess. Then there were "derbs", the word we used for marbles, and "joopeen", which roughly means dodging. This gives us "joopeen in" (without paying) and "joopeen school", a practice often curtailed by "tha joopeen mannie" or "joopeen jannie". Just a few miles away,

Dingwall appears to have a much richer variety of alternative words such as "gadgie" and "coff" (both terms for a man) and "manishee" (a woman), many of them believed to have gypsy origins.

Imagine a scenario where an Invernessian goes into a chippy to obtain their "laanch" (otherwise known as "dunnurr", as in "Ah'm no goeen home furma dunnur the day"). When they request "a block poodeen sappur an' a kon ov coke", the words are all standard English vocabulary, but their pronunciation is unique to the Inverness area. Such a request is likely to evoke a response prefixed by the standard Inverness term "Uryiz wo'een...." such as "Uryiz wo'een sal' an' vunagur?" When it comes to payment, the purchaser might exclaim "Whurze mawollut?", evoking the reassurance from his friend "Thurz it... in yer bock pockutt".

"Uryiz wo'een" is well established in Inverness and is tailor made for local Subway shops. "Uryiz wo'een le'uss?...uryiz wo'een tamatoze?.... uryiz wo'een bu'urr?.... uryiz wo'een dresseen?" Then it's up to the shop assistant to enquire "Izat evryheen fur tishnow?"... with the possible response: "Naw... ah'm needeen suheen furtha burrn."

The terms "wo'een" and "bu'urr" lead us on to another staple of the Inverness accent, the glottal (or glo'al) stop. By no means unique to the Highland Capital, this abandonment of all but initial letters "t" is commonplace here. "Ifyur no home by tena clock yur ge'een ba'ured" a threatening parent might intone. Meanwhile at the bar it might be "Whusky an' wo'urr, junn and bi'urr lemman an' two pintsa Stella Ar'wah".

Inverness speech frequently percolates into all areas of society including the NHS since for many years the "voice" in the lifts at Raigmore Hospital was locally customised, advising passengers of "Doorsh oapneen" and "Doorsh clozeen."

Moray Firth Radio has been a rich source of Invernessian intonations over the years. One very wintry morning, an announcer was heard to advise listeners that "Thursh NO Sunday paypursh in Nurrn". Of course, "takeen tha burrn ti Nurn" has been a favourite local activity ever since railway travel came to the Highland Capital. And then, one Saturday afternoon in the 1980s, the MFR sports report, giving the "dee'uls" of various Highland League matches, began to extol the scoring exploits of "Blyeeaaghart". Now that one had me confused for a while, until I remembered that my old schoolmate Billy had returned to Caley after his time at Rangers and Wigan, and that the title of "Aaghart Cassal" was similarly corrupted.

Accent also evolves with geography and the Inverness one isn't hugely dissimilar to others in the east central Highlands. And although the difference between Inverness and Dingwall will be obvious to locals, this may pass others by completely. Nairn is different again, but not radically, although you just have to cross the border into Moray and there's a sea change even when you get to "Four-ass" and more so to Elgin. Anyone who can decipher what is said in Buckie, (and indeed in Hawick) deserves huge respect. Alexa is also said to have great difficulty with Glaswegian, although – incredibly - apparently not with Invernessians.

Inverness doesn't seem to have internal variants of poshness which are perhaps more features of larger cities. This can even be detected in Aberdeen where the more affluent classes tend to draw out their vowels in slightly languid fashion. In Glasgow there seems to be a bit of a continuum ranging from classic proletarian Seeyoujimmy right through to the refaaiiined vowels of Kelvinsaiiide. And my goodness, over the years, didn't Billy Connolly steadily gentrify his delivery no end?!

During my four years in Edinburgh I became no more reconciled with the local accent there than I did with the bizarre practice of embalming chips in salt and sauce. But I did discover that in the city's more genteel areas such as Mauningsaiiide, where Miss Jean Brodie held sway, a creche isn't a childminding service but a motor accident. Meanwhile, crepe paper has got nothing to do with Christmas but can always be found in toilets. In Inverness, any variation tends to be across a continuum running from neutral to extreme.

In an earlier Inverness book, I created a conversation between George, a schoolboy, and his friend Hamish, a "bowsher" or bicycle delivery boy.
"Howyadooen Geordie boy?"
"No bad, Hame. How's yersel, like?"
"Ach yer see'een it Geord, yer see'een it."
"An how's yur bru'ur?"
"Ach he's orright. Meezals it wuz. He's back a' his work but mah u'ur bru'ur's go' it now so he's a' home wi mah mu'ur. Anyway, be'urr get on mah way. Ah've go'ah get them fush t' a wifie on Kingsmills Road an ah'm late arreddee. See ya Geord."
Some years later, "Geord" finds himself in "Tha Gelluns" where one of the clientele announces "Ah'm burshteen!" before heading straight for a door marked "Gents". Two minutes later, this person reappears through the door and exclaims:
"Geordie! Howyadooen? Ah wuz burshteen mun!"

"Ach no' bad Alecky boy. Yer see'een it, but yer blazeen again an' all, like."

It's conversations like these that set Invernessians aside from all others. Then there's the saying that "You can take the boy (girl) out of Inverness, but you can never take Inverness out of the boy." Reading through various Invernessian Facebook pages, It was impossible to miss the huge enthusiasm that exiles across the world have for what, as their home, was probably a town as opposed to the "suttee" it later became. Going "ovar tha suttee" just doesn't seem to have the same ring as "ovar tha tuwwn".

Old affinities die hard and that thought certainly helped inspire the writing of this book. This "suttee" of ours may look very different from earlier decades and few would argue that changes have all been for the better. But for so many, it's where we have our roots - and would we ever give these up?

"Yer jokeen mun!"

EPILOGUE.

This narrative of an Inverness upbringing could have been brought to a close at the end of secondary schooling but at that point, in June 1971, I still had nine months left in St Andrew Drive before our move to Holm Mills. And if there has been one constant anchor throughout this tale, it has been Dalneigh. It was on that estate that I was forged and spent many of my most formative moments, so parting company with it must also mark a conclusion here.

Although I had always looked forward to the academic challenge of university, the practical upheaval of living half the year in Edinburgh never grabbed me with quite such enthusiasm. I attribute that largely to my love of Inverness, which was in turn born out of almost 14 happy years in Dalneigh, and a happy family life.

This is probably why I never quite settled in Edinburgh as well as my friends did. I spent a minimum of time there and went home at weekends rather more often than the rest. My affinity with Inverness probably influenced in part my decision to abandon Plan A to follow up my first degree with a PhD. Instead, I went into teaching where I could be reasonably sure of getting a job in Inverness.

None of this has ever presented me with a moment of regret and I went off the idea of research anyway. Indeed, my decision to return home quickly provided me with many marvellous, unseen life opportunities, including writing books about the place. This is now my seventh.

It was during my very first hour at Pollock Halls of Residence that I suddenly realised that I was on a different course from my friends. We all arrived pretty well simultaneously one late September Saturday, checked into our halls and met up in Richard's room. All of a sudden, Richard looked about him and said with great intensity: "Well that's it, then. I live here now!", and I thought to myself "Well I have to say that I don't. I still live in Inverness and I'm only here to get a degree."

There was one very welcome home from home in Edinburgh which had a strong Dalneigh link. In the summer of 1971, Hamish MacIntyre left Dalneigh after 20 years to take up a charge at Rosehall Parish Church, just 100 yards along Dalkeith Road from Pollock Halls. At this point, Sheila and Helen were both at home at weekends and sometimes – the misappropriation of apples apparently forgiven - we would go along to their new manse on a Sunday evening.

I really didn't have any problem with the independence of no longer returning to the family home each night and having to budget for myself. Despite having had a total skive in Sixth Year, I also coped quite comfortably with the work. However, I was always counting the days until my next weekend home on the Friday afternoon train from Waverley; to be away from Inverness for more than a fortnight was a rarity. Indeed, in Third Year, one reason for choosing Business Studies as a course was that lecture times allowed me to concentrate all my 16 hours of classes into Tuesdays and Thursdays. This was hard going on these days. But it did give me a Wednesday off and, more importantly, I could take very long weekends home due to not having classes on Mondays or Fridays. And Business Studies turned out to be a commendably easy course!

On arriving at Inverness station early on a Friday

evening, I used to go straight to the Church Hall to see some of my slightly younger friends in the Boys' Brigade and Guides. Then on the Saturday night there was a chance to meet my Harriers associates in the pub. Come my later Edinburgh years, around 1973, the Hayloft in Eastgate burst on the Inverness social scene, possibly as no other venue had before.

The place would be mobbed right up to closing time and you always dreaded it being your round – not because you had to pay for it but because you knew that queueing at the bar would take you away from your drink and your company for quite a long time. My frequent companions there were Willie Junor and Brian Ledingham from the Harriers; many athletics ambitions were formulated in the extremely unhealthy environment of thick cigarette smoke and copious alcohol consumption in that packed upstairs bar. Even when I decided not to drink at all and spent a whole year consuming pints of lemonade, the Hayloft and the Barrel Vault above the Rendezvous were still favourites.

One Saturday in the Hayloft the legendary Highland Games thrower Hamish Davidson, who had briefly joined the Harriers a year previously, came up to us and produced a folded piece of paper. This, he claimed, contained cannabis which was available at a very good price. But apart from the fact that were weren't in the least interested, we also knew that Hamish, who ran a sheep farm at Cawdor, was in the habit of collecting the droppings and passing them off as The Weed.

Catching the Sunday night or Monday train back to Edinburgh was always done rather less enthusiastically than the northbound journey. I always found that return trip just a bit depressing and the strong brewery smell when we drew into Haymarket Station was a sure sign of being back in Auld Reekie. To me, that smell epitomised Edinburgh and if I ever make that journey even now, whiffing it has the strangest of unsettling effects.

University holidays often meant student jobs. Since student grants were quite generous at that time, no one I knew had employment in Edinburgh itself, but we did work during summer holidays in particular. In the break between school and university, I got a job at £10 a week and 5p commission per dozen bottles, developing sales for Bon Accord lemonade whose depot was on Anderson Street.

My boss was Tommy Robb, whose family owned the business, and his deputy in the factory was Roy Lobban who was also a great Caley supporter. Initially I was given a green pick-up truck and was sent round the Inverness houses with a couple of dozen cases of various flavours. Sales actually went very well so I made quite a lot of money in commission. Then, just turned 18, and seven months on from passing my test, I suddenly found myself promoted to a 3 ton truck which was the heaviest my licence allowed me to drive.

But that wasn't my scariest driving experience at Bon Accord. On one occasion, Tommy needed an errand run so he threw me the keys of his son Vincent's Mark 1 Cortina. In my naivety I had no idea that this thing was souped up to the nines, so I applied the accelerator normally.... only to find myself at the far end of Madras Street before I knew what had hit me!

I went back that Christmas, fortunately this time driving a van, and one of these obscure memories that strangely sticks half a century later is of sitting in the Haugh listening on the van radio to Tony Christie's recently released classic Amarillo.

At least it was a change from Rod Stewart's Maggie May which our student group had adopted as an anthem. We got into the habit of singing it everywhere we went (apart from when we serenaded Perth station with Miss American Pie) and many renditions of Maggie were given during that first, very convivial Christmas holiday back from university. It was some New Year too which enhanced my suspicion that I really do not like whisky.

Apart from the obligatory one-off pub crawl of Rose Street's then 14 establishments I drank very little at university, although I did attend the Pollock Halls Burns Supper in January 1972. The speaker was poet Norman McCaig and the whisky there, which was all too readily available on the table, finally sickened me of the stuff.

Returning to Inverness for the Easter Holidays was a sad-happy occasion. There was the delight of being home and the curiosity of moving into a new house, but these were tempered by strong twinges of regret at leaving Dalneigh.

My father again applied to house purchase the well tried principle that acquisitions are better delayed until they can be safely and comfortably afforded. He was in his early 50s before we joined the gathering flood of Dalneigh residents upgrading to owner occupancy as mortgages became more readily available. For us it was a two bedroomed bungalow at number 6, Dores Avenue, a cul de sac off Dores Road, costing around £5000, and very nice it was too. But it wasn't Dalneigh and it was a lot further both from the town and from the Harriers at the Bught.

Here it was, though. April 1972, when the Royal Scots Dragoon Guards' Amazing Grace inherited Number One from Nilsson's equally iconic Without You. The time had come to leave Dalneigh with these very tunes, possibly the latter in particular, ringing in my head.

One last look round that garden and into the wooden shed my dad had built. Driving the car out of Garage Number 6 for the last time. A final walk round St Andrew, St Fergus, St Valery and the rest of that great Dalneigh Hagiography. Memories of nicking the Minister's apples, penny bangers thrown up garden paths, Christison's penny box, football at the Back O' Kavvies', the primary school which preceded the equally formative Inverness Royal Academy.

A move from a council housing scheme to their own home is a significant change for any family but for me this departure also marked the true end of a supremely happy period of growing up, and the real beginning of adulthood.

As the years have gone by, I have found myself returning to Dalneigh rather more frequently for a drive or a run round. The memories remain crystal clear – almost exclusively happy memories too. I had the time of my life in Dalneigh, and still do in Inverness where I was made.